The mental health & w

D1635730

www.triggerpublishin

The**inspirational**series™
Overcoming adversity and thriving

Man Up Man Down
Standing Up To Suicide
BY PAUL MCGREGOR

We are proud to introduce The**inspirational**series™. Part of the Trigger family of innovative mental health books, The**inspirational**series™ tells the stories of the people who have battled and beaten mental health issues. For more information visit: www.triggerpublishing.com

THE AUTHOR

Paul McGregor is a mental health speaker, author, and the Founder of EveryMind. In 2009, Paul lost his dad to suicide – it came as a shock to everyone; there were no warning signs. At just 19 years old, Paul struggled to deal with it. He overworked, chased "success" and distracted himself from the grief. Shortly after his dad's suicide, Paul too found himself in a dark place, suffering with depression and fearing he'd follow in his dad's footsteps. With time and hard work, Paul found his way to recovery, and now shares that story in the hope that others suffering in silence will share their stories too. As a dad of two, he's also driven to normalise the conversation around mental health for the next generation. To help his children, and others know that it's okay to speak up about how they're feeling. Paul has been featured in *GQ*, *HuffPost UK*, and *The Guardian*, and appeared on *Sky News*, and *BBC News*. He continues to share his experiences and the experiences of others, standing up to the stigma that surrounds mental health, and promotes   or those who need i

014322424 4

First published in Great Britain 2018 by Trigger

Trigger is a trading style of Shaw Callaghan Ltd & Shaw Callaghan 23 USA, INC.

The Foundation Centre

Navigation House, 48 Millgate, Newark

Nottinghamshire NG24 4TS UK

www.triggerpublishing.com

Copyright © Paul McGregor 2018

British Library Cataloguing in Publication Data

A CIP catalogue record for this book is available upon request
from the British Library

ISBN: 978-1-912478-46-0

This book is also available in the following formats:

MOBI: 978-1-912478-49-1
EPUB: 978-1-912478-47-7
PDF: 978-1-912478-48-4
AUDIO: 978-1-912478-87-3

Paul McGregor has asserted his right under the Copyright,
Design and Patents Act 1988 to be identified as the author of this work

Cover design More Visual. Typeset by Fusion Graphic Design Ltd.

Printed and bound in Great Britain by Clays Ltd, Elcograf S.p.A.

Paper from responsible sources

TRIGGER™

The mental health & wellbeing publisher

www.triggerpublishing.com

Thank you for purchasing this book.
You are making an incredible difference.

Proceeds from all Trigger books go directly to
The Shaw Mind Foundation, a global charity that focuses
entirely on mental health. To find out more about
The Shaw Mind Foundation visit,
www.shawmindfoundation.org

MISSION STATEMENT

Our goal is to make help and support available for every
single person in society, from all walks of life.
We will never stop offering hope. These are our promises.

Trigger and The Shaw Mind Foundation

Creating hope for children,
adults and families

A NOTE FROM THE SERIES EDITOR

The Inspirational range from Trigger brings you genuine stories about our authors' experiences with mental health problems.

Some of the stories in our Inspirational range will move you to tears. Some will make you laugh. Some will make you feel angry, or surprised, or uplifted. Hopefully they will all change the way you see mental health problems.

These are stories we can all relate to and engage with. Stories of people experiencing mental health difficulties and finding their own ways to overcome them with dignity, humour, perseverance and spirit.

Paul explores his grief at losing his father to suicide, and the depression which he experienced afterwards. In healing himself, he had to overcome the belief that men should hide their emotions. He warns of the dangers of overworking in the name of chasing success, and challenges prevailing gender stereotypes. In particular, he speaks about how important it is for men to support each other when experiencing difficult emotion. Paul now runs a successful business, has a loving family, and he advocates for greater conversation around men's mental health. Above all, Paul's story encourages us all to open up and talk about our own mental health and emotional problems.

This is our Inspirational range. These are our stories. We hope you enjoy them. And most of all, we hope that they will educate and inspire you. That's what this range is all about.

Lauren Callaghan,
Co-founder and Lead Consultant Psychologist at Trigger

Dad. This book is for you.

Not one day passes without me wishing you were here to run alongside, to hear you laugh uncontrollably to things that really aren't funny and to hear you say those four words again: 'I'm proud of you.'

But even though I can't physically see you, even though none of these things will ever happen again, I know you're here. And I now know you're at peace.

Thank you for everything you did for me.

Disclaimer: Some names and identifying details have been changed to protect the privacy of individuals.

Trigger Warning: This book contains references to suicide.

Trigger encourages diversity and different viewpoints, and is dedicated to telling genuine stories of people's experiences of mental health issues. However, all views, thoughts, and opinions expressed in this book are the author's own, and are not necessarily representative of Trigger as an organisation.

CHAPTER 1

IMPACT

On 4th March 2009, my dad left the house, walked 15 minutes to a busy road, and stepped in front of a lorry.

He died on impact.

I was 18 years old – a month off 19 – and that was the day that changed my life.

Fuck!

Why did he do it?

My dad's suicide shocked us as a family. It shocked his friends and co-workers, and hurt so many more people.

But to you reading this, chances are my dad's suicide is just a digit. One more number added to this statistic: in the UK in 2015, 4,624 men took their own lives.

That's right … just in the UK. That tiny little speck on the world map.

This affects us all, but to the men reading this, I'd like to ask you these questions:

Isn't it time we did something about it?

Do we really need to "man up" and get a grip … or should we actually "man down" and change the way we deal with our emotions?

Is there even a right or wrong way of managing how we feel?

You may not know who I am right now, but I'm about to reveal everything to you. This book has been born out of nine years of self-reflection, realisations, and yes, mistakes. Shortly after losing my dad to suicide, I too battled with depression, anxiety, and even contemplated taking my own life. In this book, I'll share with you my fears and insecurities, and take you back to the darkest days I've ever experienced.

But I want this book to do more. And I think you can help me with that ... I want this book to stand up to suicide.

CHAPTER 2

EVERY 40 SECONDS

Actor and comedian Robin Williams, musician Kurt Cobain, fashion designer Lee (Alexander) McQueen, ex-footballer Gary Speed, singer Chester Bennington, chef Anthony Bourdain, and DJ Avicii are just a few men in the limelight who saw suicide as the only way out of the darkness.

Shockingly, someone, somewhere in the world takes their own life every 40 seconds. Just reflect on that for a minute. If the trend continues, that figure is expected to rise to one suicide every 20 seconds. You might be wondering why I only picked out men in that list above ... What a lot of people don't know is that, out of all of the suicides recorded in 2015, 75% were men. We're supposed to be the tough ones, the emotionally stable ones, but there is a devastating imbalance of men taking their own lives in comparison to women.

Simply put, as a man aged under 45, the biggest threat to my own life right now is myself. It's my mental health. It's suicide.

But I'm not neglecting women here. The rates of suicide among women are rising and depression can affect anyone. It doesn't discriminate.

No wonder so many people are oblivious to this. People just don't like talking about depression. And they definitely don't talk about suicide. It was a full six years after being personally affected by my own depression and my dad's suicide that I learnt just how huge this problem is. And if I didn't know for all that time – as someone who had been so deeply affected by these things – why should anyone else?

The statistics are shocking, but they're likely to be higher. They don't include the unrecorded suicides, or the suspicious road accidents that could be suicide. They don't include the high percentage of men dying from alcoholism and drug abuse, and they don't include the many men struggling right now with deep depression, who are contemplating taking their own lives.

We're killing ourselves on a daily basis through a never-ending list of self-sabotaging behaviours. A lot of us are drinking too much, eating badly, entering and staying in damaging relationships, working too hard in a job we don't enjoy, and creating needless stress.

This book is here to share my personal journey through depression and dealing with my dad's suicide. I'm holding nothing back: all my depression, my insecurities, the truth about my dad killing himself, and the lessons I've learnt along the way. I spent nine years being closed off, but now it's time to truly come clean.

Because things can get better. And they *will* get better if we change the way we think about mental illness …

So I'm opening up in this book with the hope that you'll do the same. I'm writing this to show you that it's okay to not be okay. I'm writing this for the men who feel like they have to wear a mask to hide how they feel, for the men who are merely existing day-to-day and struggle to get out of bed every morning. I'm writing this for the people who are fed up with the stigma that surrounds mental health and suicide. And most of all, I'm writing this for anyone who's been impacted by suicide. Whether you're aiming to get closure on why a loved one ended their own life, or whether you're a man currently struggling with depression and suicidal thoughts ... I'm hoping my honesty and vulnerability will help you.

Instances of depression are on the rise. Suicide rates are scarily high and yet we're still turning a blind eye.

It's time for change.

CHAPTER 3

BACK WHERE
IT ALL BEGAN

I was born at 2.07am on Thursday 20th April 1990, with an instinct for self-sabotage. Somehow, on my way into the world, I managed to wrap the umbilical cord around my neck, not just once, but three times.

Mum tells me of the moment the nurses excitedly told her, 'There's his head!' only to quickly follow it up with screams of, 'Don't push, don't push!' If she'd pushed, the cord would have tightened, and it could have strangled me.

The scare was short-lived and I was successfully delivered. The nurses unwrapped the cord and handed me to Mum. Looking back at old photos I had a bit of a blue tint, almost like a mini Smurf!

When we went onto the ward, one of the nurses said, 'This is the little one who nearly didn't make it.'

The strangling incident may have been a worry, but Mum remembers them being concerned about something else, 'He's got one nipple bigger than the other!'

So there I was: a little blue baby, with odd nipples, who had tried to strangle himself three times. All in all, it was a pretty dramatic entrance into the world.

They put me in an incubator (or "fish tank" as my brother remembers it) for a while – just to be on the safe side. But the near-strangling incident didn't cause any problems, the nipples were nothing to worry about, and I weighed a healthy 7lbs 11oz. There was just one problem ... I would not shit!

It took me 48 hours to have my first poo. Mum recalls them stirring things along by sticking a thermometer up my ass. I finally did the deed, and I went home two days later.

I was born into a loving family of four. Mum (Lin), Dad (Neil), my older brother of two years (Steven), and my mum's first love ... her dog, Max.

We lived in an average sized, three-bedroom semi-detached house, in a cul-de-sac in Benfleet, Essex. Mum and Dad had been childhood sweethearts, and married when Mum was 19 and Dad was 23. A couple of years later, Steven came along, and then, two years after that, there was me.

I knew that Mum and Dad loved us dearly, and I'm so grateful for it. They honestly showed us the kind of love and affection that every child deserves.

The early years of my life rushed by, but so many memories remain. I smile when I think back to all those times playing in the garden with Steve, the family time we enjoyed in the evenings, and the times when Mum would entertain us when we went to watch Dad run in races most weekends.

Steve was a big role model to me, and I always looked up to him. With just two years between us, I watched his every move and tried my hardest to copy him. Like the time we went swimming – I was still young and learning, but Steve was a strong swimmer. I stood on the side of the pool, ripped off my armbands, and shouted 'I want to swim like Steven!' I jumped in the pool, kicked my legs, fluttered my arms, and sank. Fortunately, Mum came swimming to the rescue.

It didn't take me long to learn how to swim though, and I felt like I learnt lots of other things quickly. Because I looked up to Steve so much and tried to do everything he did, I was riding a bike at four and settled into school easily. After a slight wobble ...

In my first year, Mum remembers the times she dropped me at school in the mornings, only for me to cry endlessly because I didn't want her to leave. We were both very close to Mum. She used to walk away with tears in her eyes, but afterwards I settled in pretty quickly.

In my early years, people would probably have defined me as a sensitive but friendly and loving boy, who was extremely attached to his parents, and looked up to his older brother. Looking back, I can see some of the habits, mannerisms and behaviours I was inheriting from my family. I was slowly starting to become me.

Even though I made friends, enjoyed playing with others, and had a good imagination, I struggled with confidence. I was extremely shy and I remember always shrinking away from any form of involvement in the annual school play. That's probably because of the time when I had my first and only involvement in the play, aged six. I walked on stage, dressed head-to-toe in a teddy bear costume, faced the audience, and burst into tears. The teacher waved Mum on stage to come and get me, and I watched the rest of the show from her lap.

Not so long ago, I wouldn't have been able to tell you that I cried like a baby while dressed as a teddy bear! It would have made me feel too vulnerable. But now I know it doesn't matter! I know that talking about these things is always okay.

Both Mum and Dad were extremely friendly people. They would even go so far as to refrain from expressing their own opinions to please others. As I got older, I started integrating well at school and making lots of friends. And yes, for better or worse, I definitely inherited my parents' traits and started holding back on expressing my opinions too.

My ego started to grow once I started senior school. It's crazy to look back now and think how big I thought I was at age 11. I was an avid footballer and made it into the first team at school. Then, after school, I'd put on my Liverpool kit, lace up my boots, and play football some more.

I was averagely smart, often being in the top half of the groups for ability across the board, but sport was my thing. I spent nearly every day after school doing some form of sport, not just football but rugby, athletics, or just running laps of the field. I knew I was good at sport, so I put the hours in. But I needed that affirmation. I wouldn't have believed it if I hadn't been told I was good at sport. My ego may have been growing, but I was still quite sensitive and lacking in confidence. If someone told me I couldn't do something I'd take their word for it. And if I didn't enjoy a subject, I wouldn't apply much effort to it. Sport was my comfort zone and the sports centre was where I spent most of my time.

As I got older and moved into my late teens, I thought more about what my life actually looked like. I think it looked different, depending on your perspective:

The outside perception?

I was cool. I was friends with the "cool kids" and played for most of the sports teams. I always had a girlfriend or some kind of love interest, and my home life was perfect. Mum and Dad were still together, we lived in a nice house in a nice location, and I was also pretty smart. I never got into fights and from the outside it looked like school life was perfect. In fact, I was sitting in a business lesson when one of the boys told me how perfect my life was and reeled off all the same reasons. On paper it was hard to disagree with him, but to me it didn't *feel* perfect.

The inside perception?

I put on a front; I played a role to protect my insecurities, often playing the joker to stop others putting me down. I worried about what others thought of me, how I looked, what I said, and what I did, and I was always intimidated by others. I remember waking up one morning with a huge spot on my forehead and I was so worried about the potential abuse I would get that I pretended I was ill and didn't go to school for two days. I don't think Mum knows about that even now. Sorry, Mum!

I consistently worried about what other people thought of me and I tried to protect the identity I'd created to keep me popular. I played too much football because that's how I felt secure. I may not have been the best in the school, but I was one of the best and I knew that no one else could put me down.

To cover up my sensitivity at school, I was playing the tough guy a bit too much; I was acting cool and looking down on others. But living with the daily fear of worrying what others thought of me and playing a role that wasn't really me was starting to cripple me. It stopped me from enjoying school life to the full. Don't get me wrong, the laughter and funny stories outweigh the bad times, and I'm still good friends with plenty of my friends from school. But I was feeling increasingly aware that the different roles we play in life don't always sit too well together.

I was reaching out and finding my place in life in other ways too. I had a love for hip-hop and UK garage. I started writing music, making beats, and rapping and MC'ing. Looking back, I cringe a little bit, but I really wasn't that bad at it. (Maybe others would say different!)

I started at about 12. It was just for fun with a few mates. Dad bought me my first turntables for Christmas and I invested in more equipment as time went on. I started recording whenever I got the chance, and was even approached by an independent UK hip-hop label from Cornwall. They sent me a mini agreement to release an EP through them. A record deal at 15 seemed like a dream come true. I went on to record the EP and they funded it. Over the space of about two months it sold around 500 copies and I made about £3.00 per CD. I entered a competition to rap/sing over two songs by the English singer/rapper Plan B. I made it to the final five before it went to a public vote. I placed second behind Maverick Sabre, who went on to get signed and have a Top 10 album. We went to see Maverick Sabre at the O2 Academy a few years ago. There were a few thousand people there and "what if ..." did cross my mind.

It all stopped when I was about 18, just before I lost Dad. I had a real passion for it, but I couldn't see myself rapping for the rest of my life. I think my insecurities and low self-esteem held me back too. I was never one to push myself; I was always embarrassed to share my songs and I always listened to that one piece of criticism over the majority of compliments.

My entrepreneurial spirit developed early too. At about age 14, I started buying branded clothes off eBay and selling them to people at school. Because I was so young I needed an adult's permission so I asked Mum if I could use her name and card – and I promised I'd pay her back.

I'd buy a tracksuit for £25 and sell it to someone at school for £40. I'd pay Mum back the £25 and keep the £15. After a while, I started ordering in branded and unbranded clothing from suppliers in China too. I set up an eBay shop to sell them. On average I sold three a day and every few days I would hold up the Post Office queue with my little pile of parcels. It made me a nice little profit to feed my expensive tastes in football boots, Nickelson polo shirts, and Burberry socks (all you late 80s and early 90s babies will know!).

With Dad being supportive of my entrepreneurial spirit but traditional in the sense that he wanted me and Steve to go out and get a job early, I secured my first job at Iceland (the supermarket, not the country!). From the age of 16, I worked there, part-time, alongside going to college. I was only making around £4.00 an hour, but at quieter times I would sit at the tills, planning out my eBay business on the back of till receipts. My boss was very laid back, and I worked there with a friend from school and two other guys who were the same age. We were all very different, but we had a lot of fun. Typically, the supermarket job and the eBay sales funded my yearly "mates' holidays" as well as driving lessons and a ridiculous amount of McDonalds!

My memories of me, Steve, Mum, and Dad, all together as a family, still make me happy. My childhood wasn't perfect, but no upbringing is. And perhaps most importantly, I've been able to reflect on the experiences I had and understand myself more. I know that a lot of who I am today is a result of how I lived my early years.

I can't thank Mum and Dad enough for the love and support they gave me on my journey. They always kept us in line but let us learn from our own mistakes too. I'll never forget the time I was around 13 and I'd just tried smoking. None of my family smoked and in reality I only did it to try to be "cool". I was walking home with Steve and my best friend Spencer, and Spencer and I shared half a cigarette. Did we enjoy it? No. Did we think we were cool? Of course we did.

I walked in the front door with Steve, and Mum immediately demanded to know, 'Who's been smoking?' Because he was two years older, she expected it to be him. When you live in a non-smoking house it's very easy to detect smoke. She sniffed Steve and sniffed his fingers. She then did the same with me and broke down in tears. She couldn't believe I had been smoking. She didn't shout at me and she didn't ground me; she told me she was disappointed. I was so afraid she was going to tell Dad, but I don't know if she ever did.

I never smoked again after that day. It wasn't that I was scared of Mum and Dad; it was because I respected them so much. I wanted to make them proud, I wanted to impress them. I never, ever wanted to upset them. I only hope I can bring my children up in the same way, giving them the love and guidance they need. And I hope they will respect me like I respected my mum and dad.

We know that our childhood defines a lot of our characteristics and personality as we get older. But sometimes it's difficult to piece all the bits together: why do some of the things that happen in our childhood make us act in a certain way when other things don't?

It all starts in childhood: the way we're conditioned by parents who were conditioned by their parents, and whose parents were conditioned by their parents. After all, we're all victims of victims.

Looking back, Dad was someone whose attention I constantly craved. He had an aura about him and whenever he was there he'd give me his attention. But he spent a lot of time not being there. He had to stay busy and spent a lot of time doing things he had to do. He worked hard as an engineer, leaving the house early every working day. He got home around 5.00pm, spent a bit of time with us, and then worked some more. He'd trained as a physiotherapist and saw private physio clients every evening. At weekends we'd spend time together, but it would mostly revolve around what Dad wanted to do. Holidays were my most cherished moments as these were the times when we had Dad's full attention.

He was a sensitive and caring Dad. He inspired me to work hard and strive to do more in life, but was very careful that I should try and live a stress-free life. I only realised that later. At times when I'd be worried about something at school or struggling with football, Dad would have an answer. He once drew out Maslow's Hierarchy of Needs for me as he tried to explain why I wasn't feeling motivated. He even tried to get me and Steve to meditate with him when we went camping, to help us keep calm. Whenever I spoke to him about my problems, he would say, 'Follow your heart and not your head.'

I had a close bond with Dad, and his sensitivity and caring behaviour made me feel safe around him, but he could switch quite quickly. If I had a bad game of football, he'd be sure to tell me, and he'd often reference how Grandad would've treated him if he'd had a bad game.

Looking back, my dad seemed to be pushed and pulled to and from what it took for him to be a "man". We knew that he was a sensitive man who seemed open with his emotions, but he was also my grandad's son. And my grandad was very "old school" – he was from the generation that went through war and poverty. My grandad isn't a nasty man in any way, he was just brought up to be a tough, no-nonsense man – and that's how he tried to raise my dad.

I think my dad questioned his role as a man on many occasions. What was the right way to be a dad? A husband? A son? What was the right way to deal with the difficult things in life – the things we didn't even know he was struggling with?

That stiff upper lip attitude to dealing with emotional pain served my grandad throughout his life, but it didn't seem to serve my dad.

On paper, he had everything. A loving wife, two sons, a mum and dad, and an abundance of friends. He was physically healthy and was an avid runner. He was studying for a psychology degree in what little spare time he had, and that was on top of his full-time and part-time jobs. He read self-help books and he meditated; he once said that he tried to take a holistic approach to life. He wouldn't even take a paracetamol to cure a headache.

On the outside, he was strong, committed, and focused. But inside, there was a different narrative going on …

CHAPTER 4

SURROUNDED BY SUICIDE

At some point in your life you'll be affected by suicide. Whether it's a family member, a friend, or a friend of a friend, you will be exposed to suicide.

Seriously.

That's bad enough. But what's even worse is that we try to avoid even talking about it. We openly talk about illness, we openly talk about death, but we try to avoid talking about mental health or suicide. No one whispers, 'He died of a heart attack,' but there seems to be a need to whisper, 'He took his own life.'

Depression is on the rise and people are still afraid to talk about it. Someone very close to you could be dealing with depression right now. Would you even know?

We all "have" mental health.

There are around 6,000 deaths by suicide in the UK each year and, for each death, research suggests that each suicide profoundly affects the lives of around 135 people. That equates to over 800,000 people bereaved and affected by suicide in the UK each year.

Suicide bereavement has devastating consequences, with 9% of people bereaved by suicide going on to make a suicide attempt themselves and 8% dropping out of work or education.

The lack of support for mental health in general, with all of the statistics pointing to a big issue, is scary. The lack of support for people who have been bereaved by suicide needs to change.

I personally never really thought about mental health, I never thought about depression and I didn't even consider looking into causes of suicide. Until my dad took his life. And now I'm ready to tell you the whole story ...

CHAPTER 5

THE ACCIDENT

I'd seen my dad cry before but this was different.

He wasn't himself.

It was one of my last days working at my part-time job in Iceland; I'd just got my first full-time job on an IT help desk.

Dad was working nights at the time so I arranged to meet him after my shift in the afternoon.

It was a bright day, the sun shone, and I was feeling genuinely excited to start the next chapter in my life.

When I got home to see him, he seemed off, not like his normal self at all. Distant. He sat at the dining table browsing on his laptop and didn't greet me in the way he normally would.

Prior to this, Dad had seemed to be doing well. He'd had some life changes to deal with though. He'd been made redundant from the job he'd been in most of his life and was now working nights in a different field. He'd lost a bit of money through shares he'd bought before the stock market crashed; he also had to cope with his mum being diagnosed with cancer. But this was stuff that Dad seemed to be dealing with. He seemed to be okay.

I'd never really seen him struggle. He'd always seemed to handle everything so well.

But his behaviour made me feel unwanted. I was going to spend some time with him and he didn't seem interested.

What was going on?

I felt like leaving him alone but as Dad stood up and approached me, I saw the pain in his eyes. Not tears … pain. He started to talk and even the sound of his voice was different. His posture was slouched and he just seemed so deflated.

I asked if he was okay and he nodded with a half-smile. Then, finally, he hugged me. Like he normally would. I remember him holding me tighter than normal and that made me feel uneasy. I didn't know what was going on.

I don't remember the conversation we had. I think I was more confused and worried about how he was acting to pay attention to what he was actually saying. I do remember him showing me his briefcase though, the briefcase that held all of his financial documents. At the time it didn't feel like a warning sign. I knew he had them and I thought he was just making conversation.

Everything just seemed off but I knew that tomorrow he'd be fine. I went to sleep that night with no worries at all, thinking: *He's my dad, he's strong.* I thought that I'd been misreading the situation.

I was wrong.

Things didn't get any better over the next few days. He called Mum and asked her to meet him at a nearby car park. When she arrived, he was sitting in his car in the pitch black, crying. She got in the car with him and tried to console him, while he tried to tell her how he was feeling.

It didn't feel like something that should be happening, but I still knew it would get better.

Later, he went to the doctors and explained just how confused he was feeling about what was causing it. The doctor gave him some antidepressants.

My dad depressed? It still didn't make sense. But I trusted the medicine would help him get out of the funk he was in. Because that's all it was. I still believed that.

In the days that followed, we were all on a huge rollercoaster of emotions. Each morning I'd text or speak to Dad to ask him how he was doing, and he'd tell me he was feeling better. But there was always something he did or something he said that didn't really fit with him feeling better.

Dad had promised to take me car shopping and told me that he was going to help me buy a new one after I'd written off my first car. He was directing me to the car dealership, but we got lost a few times as he wasn't really paying attention to the roads. He was spending a lot of time on his phone. The whole time we were there he seemed so distant. He was panicking at things that wouldn't normally have bothered him at all.

We popped into the shops afterwards to get some dinner and I left him to go down another aisle. After just a minute or two, I went back to the aisle I'd left Dad in and saw that he was no longer there. I went to the next aisle to try and find him. Suddenly, he came running up to me with panic in his eyes and pulled me towards him. 'I thought I'd lost you,' he said. I was 18 now – an adult – and I never would have expected to see that sort of pure panic in my dad's eyes.

We were all starting to get extremely worried about him.

My first day at my new job had arrived and I spent the full day training. I'd been in contact with Mum throughout the day and she was keeping in touch with Dad. He'd gone back to the doctors as he didn't feel like the antidepressants were doing any good; the doctor told him to double his dose to see if that helped.

My first day went well, but I was still worried about Dad. Everything was still extremely raw; it had only been around 10 days since that day I'd found Dad behaving so differently. When I spoke to him about it afterwards, he seemed okay.

As I finished my second day at work I arrived home to find Mum and Steve in the kitchen. Mum told us that Dad had called an ambulance for himself. She said he had been feeling suicidal.

Suicidal?

None of us could understand just how extreme this was getting. We knew he had called for an ambulance and been taken to hospital, and Mum said we'd pick him up and take him home. But it had been a few hours and none of us could reach him when we tried calling. Panic started to set in. Mum rang my nan and grandad (my dad's mum and dad) and they came up to the house. I drove up to the hospital with Steve to see if we could find him. And all the while we continued to phone, hoping he'd pick up. He had never been very good with his mobile and hardly ever used it, so we thought he must have just left it in his pocket.

As we approached the hospital in the car, we noticed that there was a lot of traffic built up on the other side of the road. It was early evening so at first we just assumed it was rush hour traffic. But as we got closer, we could see that there had been an accident. We'd later find out that it had involved Dad.

We parked up in the hospital and continued to try to call him. Still nothing. We walked to the main entrance and asked around. We got sent to Accident and Emergency, where he would have been taken, and again asked if anyone had seen him. The receptionist at A&E told us that he had been there, but he'd left shortly after arriving.

I called on the mobile again and this time I got an answer, but it wasn't my dad's voice. It was a policeman. 'What relation are you?' he asked. 'I'm his son,' I said. 'I'm sorry to say this, but your dad has been in a serious road accident,' he said. There was a sympathetic tone to his voice, but it was hard to listen. He went on to tell me that Dad was currently being seen by the doctors and he couldn't really tell me much more. He did explain how serious his injuries were, and one more thing ... It was what we were all dreading to hear ...

'Witnesses say he stepped into the road.'

Eventually, we pieced it all together. Dad had been taken to A&E and waited to be seen. He had waited for a while and then walked to the main road just outside the hospital. He had been seen standing by the side of the road, about 150 metres from the roundabout. He'd crossed the road to the side where the oncoming cars would be speeding up. And then, as a van had approached, gaining speed after the roundabout, my dad had stepped into the road, right in front of it.

The cause of the accident on the other side of the road ... it had been Dad.

Fuck.

Mum arrived at the hospital quickly afterwards, with my nan and grandad. She'd waited with them; I'm sure she'd been trying to reassure them that everything would be okay. Nan had been battling cancer for just over 18 months and she was starting to get weaker. I'll never forget the sadness I saw in her eyes that day. It was like nothing I'd ever seen before.

We all hugged; my mum was tearful but trying to hold it together for us, and the shock surrounded us all.

Hours of waiting felt like decades. We just wanted to know what was going on. Finally, there was news ...

The doctors had done all they could; Dad was stable, but on a life support machine. He had hit his head so hard that there was a blood clot on his brain. He needed surgery, urgently. He was going to be transferred to a hospital about 40 minutes away to have the clot removed.

They kept telling us that there was nothing we'd be able to do now. It was a waiting game. Grandad wanted to take Nan home, so after some time of being told that Dad was stable, we drove them home and went to check on the family dog, Charlie. None of us knew what to say or do. They'd told us to go home and wait, but Mum and I went back to the hospital to see if we could get any more news or hopefully see Dad.

It was late when we arrived, around 10.00pm, and the hospital was extremely quiet. A nurse invited us in to see Dad. We walked in and couldn't believe what we saw. Dad was battered from the accident and lying absolutely still. The machine was doing all his breathing for him.

The nurse looked grimly serious and her tone of voice wasn't reassuring. She was preparing us for the worst; she said it was highly unlikely that Dad would pull through the operation. I stood by the bed with Mum, tears running down our faces as we both tried to get our heads around what was happening.

There was nothing we could do, nothing we could say to change what had happened. Just seeing Dad in that condition was unbearable; we leant in and told him everything was going to be okay. We couldn't stay there any longer and as we left, the nurse told us we'd hear from the hospital when they had news. She left us in no doubt that it probably wasn't going to be good news.

That night was the worst night of all of our lives. Back at home, we went to our own rooms, but as soon as we heard crying, we all huddled together in Mum's room, where we waited for the call.

They operated on Dad that night and the surgeon managed to remove the blood clot. They rang to tell us that he was in an induced coma because of the injuries and we could go to see him in a few hours.

We travelled up together in near silence. The phone call was positive; they said the surgery had gone better than they'd expected. But we had never seen anyone in a coma and none of us knew what to expect.

We walked through the double doors and were directed to Dad's bed. His hair had been shaved off and his head was bandaged to cover the huge operation scar across his head. He was attached to multiple wires.

'He won't be able to respond; he possibly won't be able to hear you, but you can speak to him.'

We didn't know what to say. We didn't even know if he'd be able to hear anything we said to him. At home it felt like we'd spent the entire time trying to piece together everything that was going on, trying to hold on to the hope that he would be okay, but also fearing the worst. But when we saw him, reality hit. Hard. This was serious.

We looked at each other, not really knowing what to do. We held his hand and spoke softly to him. We kept telling him over and over that he was going to be okay. I think this reassurance was also for us – we were just trying to reassure ourselves that he'd pull through.

Days passed. A few of his friends visited, but there were still no signs of improvement. We were constantly reassured by the doctors and nurses that it was normal, but they also told us they didn't know how he would be when (and if) he came round.

On the fifth morning, we got an early morning call from the hospital. Dad was awake. We were so excited travelling to see him; we would finally be able to talk to him. Even if he couldn't speak, he'd be able to squeeze our hands back. He would know we were there for him. We were hopeful, but still prepared for the worst …

As we approached, we could see Dad sitting up in bed and he smiled as he saw us walking towards him. We couldn't believe it. The change was phenomenal. I had thought that my dad might be gone for ever. But there he was, my dad – he had been given back to me.

As I write this, I can still feel the emotions that ran through me. Joy, happiness, relief. I'd truly prepared myself for the worst when the accident first happened. And as every day of him not waking from his coma had passed, my fears had increased. Just seeing him sitting up smiling was the best feeling.

We hugged, we cracked a few jokes about his scar and his shaved head, and everything seemed okay. But when we spoke about the accident and about him attempting to take his own life, he seemed confused. He kept reassuring us that he wouldn't even consider suicide. He wondered if the medication he'd been on might have caused it.

I never expected him to deny it, but when he reassured us that he would never normally have done it, I believed him. I believed everything my dad told me. The antidepressants he was on gave "suicidal thoughts" as a potential side effect. My dad – who never took much medication – had been told to double his dose; so it probably wasn't surprising that he'd encountered such extreme side effects from taking them. It made sense. I truly believed what he was saying.

With his reassurance that the medication was to blame, and the additional reassurance that he was feeling better and acting like the man we all knew, we walked away happy. The nightmare was over.

CHAPTER 6

THE DAY
MY DAD DIED

Dad spent a few weeks in the hospital as he recovered from the surgery. The day he was finally let out of hospital was a day of joy. It had been a long road of recovery but as we sat together as a family, enjoying fish and chips, I thought everything was going to be okay.

As the weeks passed though, Dad started to act differently. His behaviour was unpredictable and he still seemed depressed. Eventually, he admitted himself into the mental health unit based in the local hospital; he knew now that he really needed help. I had to learn to accept that too.

At the time, I thought a mental health unit was for loonies and I still clung onto the belief that suicide was a selfish act. But the truth is, my dad was depressed and he *had* tried to kill himself. I still had a lot to learn.

My dad was in and out of the unit and spent a good few months being monitored. I'll never forget the many occasions we visited Dad at the mental health unit throughout his depression. It was an eye-opening place. There was a young guy in there who seemed to have so much manic energy. A lot of what he said didn't make any sense. But he could be funny and he often made our visits more enjoyable.

'I tried shagging your dad last night,' was one of the things he said to me as I walked in to visit Dad.

I laughed and so did Dad. When we visited Dad on Christmas Day, the young guy bounded up to me and asked to whisper something in my ear. His presence and high energy made me feel like I had to agree, alongside my people-pleasing behaviours, so I approached cautiously. He went as if to whisper but instead licked the inside of my ear, laughing after he did it. That was the same day he proposed to me. He wrote on the back of an old photo of him, *Marry me*.

We never did tie the knot.

That Christmas, he shared some of his old photos – photos of him travelling, photos of his family and friends, photos in which he seemed not just happy but completely present and aware. He was obviously younger in the photos, in his late teens to early twenties, but the difference compared to the current version of him was shocking. He was removed from the unit a few days later and taken to a more secure facility. They just "couldn't handle him" any more.

One patient walked round murmuring things like, 'I should have killed him,' while listening to loud music on his headphones. Others made as much noise as they possibly could and argued with the nurses. Some just sat there in a complete daze, refusing to take any medication.

With everything going on with all of the other patients, one thing was for certain – my dad didn't look like he belonged there. He was being monitored by the nurses and given daily medication. They encouraged him to take part in group activities and gave me opportunities to speak to therapists. But apart from that, he often kept himself to himself, doing crosswords and word searches, and even managed to build the present that we gave him – a model of a small wooden windmill.

To us, it didn't look like he belonged there. We wanted him out, we wanted him home, we wanted him back to normal, but we knew he was safe in the unit.

I don't know what happened to the other patients. The guy who proposed to me, the guy muttering violent phrases to himself, even the woman who walked around every day with thick sun cream on her face. All I know is, my dad, who seemed to be the quiet one, the one you'd label "normal" ... wasn't, in fact, "normal". In the end, he was the one who couldn't handle it, who became so mentally ill that he felt as if walking in front of a lorry was his only option.

Dad was discharged slowly, to give him time to adapt. I remember meeting him in the unit and we were allowed to walk to the main hospital where we had dinner in the restaurant. We sat there chatting, just me and him. He didn't seem 100% better, but he was a lot better than he had been. After that, we walked back to the unit to sign him in for the night. It felt like things were looking up.

On the day he was fully discharged he seemed to be managing things better. His behaviour was still "off" at times, but he came to watch me play football, he went golfing with his friend, he went to watch the occasional running session, and he continued taking his medication and seeing his therapist.

But it started getting harder. It got to the point where we didn't know how to behave around him, we didn't know how he would be feeling or what he would do each day, and it was tiring. We had seen him slowly getting better in the unit and we had been so hopeful.

There were many occasions where Dad would be spotted walking in unexpected places, around busy roads. There was one occasion when one of his running friends had spotted him quite far from home, again walking near a busy road. He picked him up, rang Mum, and dropped him off at home. There were other times too where Dad would do something extremely out of character and, afterwards, would want to go to the mental health unit. So we'd take him back and he'd come out again a little while later.

It was my brother's birthday on 22nd February and we went out for a family meal – me, Mum, Dad, Steve, Nan and Grandad. Dad seemed okay but something wasn't quite right. Mum remembers him winking at her across the table, something he had only ever done when they first met each other. He also got annoyed at Grandad for complaining about his steak not being cooked enough. Again, my dad wouldn't normally have challenged Grandad like that.

'At least I saw Steve turn 21,' Dad said to Mum.

'What do you mean? You'll see Paul turn 21 as well,' Mum replied.

Was Dad playing an act? Was he actually feeling better or was he just trying to behave as if he was feeling better?

A few more days passed and Dad went to stay with Nan and Grandad. We were open to whatever he wanted to do – we just wanted him to get better. I went to visit him with Mum one Saturday, after Grandad told us that Dad hadn't been great. Looking back, my nan and grandad never really understood the seriousness of his mental state. Maybe it was their generation, but even with everything that had happened I still think they thought it was just a "phase" and he'd snap out of it.

I went upstairs to see him. He was curled up on the bed with nothing on. He'd been there all day. He didn't even notice when I walked in.

'Dad, are you okay?' I asked. No reply. His face was buried in a pillow.

I wondered what he would have done if I had been in that situation. What would he have said to me? I adjusted my body language and started to speak louder.

'Come on, Dad, let's get up! Let's go downstairs.' I guess I was trying to motivate him, trying to kick some life into him. Dad was always the one giving me life lessons, motivating me, and trying to help me deal with the challenges that children face as they grow up. But now, here I was, trying to help him.

'What do you want to do, Dad?' I asked. I remember his response quite vividly, and he said it again and again, 'I don't want to be here, I want to die.'

He'd never really admitted it openly before. This was the first time I'd heard him say he wanted to kill himself.

He got up then and started putting his running clothes on. I asked him what he was doing and he replied quite innocently, 'I'm going for a run.' After just telling me he wanted to kill himself, I suspected that a "run" meant something else.

I stopped him. I calmly put my hands on his shoulders to show I wanted to help, and gently restrained him to stop him stepping out of the bedroom door. He didn't like that. It was as if I was the one thing standing in his way.

Slowly he clenched his fist and started to raise it towards me.

My dad had never smacked me as a child. He had never been strict, never violent, and I don't think he'd ever had a physical confrontation with anyone in his life before.

As he stood there, clenched fist aimed towards me, I looked into his eyes. He wasn't my dad. Those eyes looking back at me – it was as if I had never seen them before. They were filled with anger, resentment, and pain.

He unclenched his fist and sat on the bed. My real dad was in there somewhere. He said to me again, 'I just want to die.'

I didn't know it then, but later I found out that something similar had happened before. Just before he had been sectioned, Mum said he had raised his fist to her, but he hadn't followed through. He had never actually been violent towards her.

Mum had gone upstairs to give him some space and to get away from him, and then she'd heard him on the phone to the emergency services, saying he felt suicidal and violent towards his wife. The ambulance and police turned up and took him into the mental health unit. Again, this violent behaviour was completely abnormal for my dad. We knew that the sensitive and caring person we all loved was still in there somewhere.

I went downstairs and called an ambulance. Dad needed help.

We all went up to keep him calm until the ambulance arrived. Our hope was that he'd be taken straight into Basildon Hospital, which had the mental health unit he'd been based in for a while. It wasn't far, just 20 minutes in the car. But when the ambulance arrived we were told he was being taken to Southend A&E so they could assess him.

Assess him? Again?! He'd attempted suicide a few months ago, spent nearly two months in the Basildon Mental Health Unit, and got discharged when he started to recover. Why did he need to be assessed again?

We were told it was policy and that he was to be taken to Southend. I followed the ambulance in the car and when I got into A&E I saw him just sitting there ... entirely on his own.

History was starting to repeat itself. The last time he had been left in A&E to wait he had walked out, gone to the nearest road, and stepped in front of a van. I could feel the anger rising; shouldn't they have been dealing with this differently?

We later found out from his reports that he had tried opening the back door of the ambulance on numerous occasions while they were driving and they'd had to restrain him. Surely that should have told them how serious this was. Why had he then been allowed to walk into a busy room and been told to sit there all alone?

It was almost like they had no respect for my dad. As if they thought this was something he could control, or something he just needed to snap out of. Maybe if he came in with physical signs of pain, blood, or limbs out of alignment, he'd have received the attention he deserved.

I sat with him for about 20 minutes, mostly in silence, until we were called in.

The first person we saw asked some pretty generic questions. They were just pre-screening him for the "expert". But it was all beginning to feel like too much for me – I had to speak up. 'Don't you know all of this? He attempted suicide a few months ago and he's been through recovery in the Basildon Mental Health Unit,' I said. She told me, 'We have no records of it, because we're not Basildon Hospital.'

Once I told her about the past (because my dad wasn't going to) we got passed through to another waiting room. This time it was just us, on a comfy sofa, waiting to be seen.

Again we sat in silence for most of it, but I remember Dad being very tender. He held my hand, nestled up to me, and we shared the occasional joke.

A lady walked in, the "expert", to discuss the problems my dad was facing. She was nice, compassionate, and very softly spoken. She asked Dad how he was feeling and he replied simply, 'fine'. He had already begun to "change back". He wasn't the same person he had been back at Nan and Grandad's.

I got asked to leave the room because she wanted to assess Dad one-to-one. So I sat back in the waiting room, while she talked to Dad for 10–15 minutes. Afterwards, she came and sat down next to me, 'After speaking with your Dad I think he's okay to go home. He seems to be a lot better now.'

I laughed. I was never one to get angry – I was a sensitive 18-year-old. I was a people pleaser and didn't like confrontation. But something else took over. 'You're joking, right?'

She could see the anger and exhaustion in me. But she carried on. 'After assessing him, he seems to be okay, and he's saying he just wants to go home to be with his family,' she said.

If this was the first time it had happened I would have accepted it and taken him home. Dad did want to be with his family, he loved us; but this time it was different.

'Of course he's saying that. A few hours ago he told me he wanted to die. He told me he wanted to kill himself,' I said.

'Oh, he never said that,' she replied.

I told her all of it. About everything that had happened over the last few months: his attempted suicide, his breakdown, his time in the mental health unit.

Again, she had no knowledge of any of it. *Don't these people talk?* I thought.

After speaking to me she decided (or I persuaded her) that Dad should be taken back to the mental health unit. And, after the paperwork was completed, they asked if I wanted to drive him back there.

I told them no. Dad was suicidal; if he did try to jump out of the car or try to harm himself, it'd finish me. I didn't want to see that. So they said he would have to wait for transport and it could take a while. We went through to the waiting ward and Dad was given a bed. I sat next to him and he curled up into the same position I'd found him in at Nan and Grandad's, his face in the pillow.

I called Mum and she was obviously upset. I felt hopeless; it felt like there was absolutely nothing I could do for him. We all felt that. When things seemed to be getting better, they quickly got worse. An older couple looked over at us. 'Has your mate had too much to drink?' the old guy asked, chuckling slightly.

'Yeah,' I chuckled back. People had often told us we looked alike and he was always told he looked young, but really?! I wondered what their reaction would be if I'd told them, 'It's my dad actually and he's here because he wants to kill himself.'

Time went on, hours passed ... still nothing. When I asked how long it would be, they couldn't give me a definitive answer.

I felt like my dad wasn't seen as a priority and he'd be the last one to be transported. No one else came to see him and we sat there in silence.

I was mentally drained and exhausted. We had been waiting for a good four hours with no sign of any transport. I wanted to go home to see Mum. I'd also made plans to go out that evening, which I wanted to stick to. So many questions crossed my mind: Should I stay with him? Could I trust that they'd get him transport? Could I even trust them to keep an eye on him? I knew I could've left at any time, but my lack of trust in how they were dealing with him kept me there longer. I went to the desk and asked them to move my dad to the front. They agreed and moved him to a bed opposite their desk. That made it easier for me to go home, knowing that they would keep an eye on him. I kissed him, hugged him, and told him I loved him.

He got transported to Basildon Mental Health Unit a few hours later.

The next day, I called the unit to speak to Dad. The lady who answered was very abrupt with me and told me to wait while she went to find him. When Dad got on the phone he spoke softly and cried like I'd never heard him cry before. He couldn't handle the way he was feeling. He couldn't handle being back there, feeling as if he was back to square one.

We weren't allowed to see him over the weekend while they assessed him and we just assumed he'd be taken back onto the unit for ongoing day care. But while I was at work on Monday, they called Grandad and asked him to go and pick Dad up. When I found out, I couldn't believe it. Pick him up? There was no way he could be feeling better. There was no way that he could be sufficiently mentally stable to come out. I think Dad knew that Grandad would pick him up without question. Steve, Mum and I couldn't know what he was going through but we knew he wasn't ready to come home this time. We would have challenged his decision.

Nevertheless, Nan and Grandad went to pick him up and took him back to their house. I went around after work and found him lying on the sofa. He still seemed dazed, vacant, and not himself.

'Your dad isn't going to be the same as he was,' he said to me.

I sat on the opposite side of the room looking at him. I knew something wasn't right. I had a sinking feeling in my stomach. Something kept telling me to put him in the car and take him back. I knew he wasn't ready to be out, but I didn't do anything. I couldn't do anything.

'I think you should go back to hospital,' I said. 'I'll be fine,' he replied.

That day haunts me. It was the last day I saw him. The last day I touched him. The last day I got to tell him I loved him.

On Tuesday 4th March 2009, I drove to work, desperately hoping that Dad would have a good day. I spoke to Grandad throughout the day; I spoke with Mum and Steve, and we all wanted to try something else to help him.

Just after lunch I called Grandad and asked how Dad was. They had some family members over and were planning to go out for lunch, but they knew Dad wouldn't be up for it.

'He's okay,' he told me, 'he's just gone for a walk to get some air.'

My heart sank and I feared the worst. Maybe Dad really had just gone for a walk, but a strong part of me was telling me something else ...

An hour passed and I rang again, desperately hoping he'd be back. He wasn't. Another hour passed and still nothing. This wasn't good.

Maybe he'd just got lost? Maybe he'd walked to the mental health unit? Maybe he'd gone to a friend's house? There were so many places he could be, but there was one place I feared the most.

I drove home from work early and got stuck in the usual rush hour traffic. Mum and Steve were already on their way to Nan and Grandad's so that we could all go to look for him.

I was the last one to get there and Dad still wasn't back. Grandad and Steve had gone to the local police station with a photo of Dad, hoping they could help us to find him.

That's when they knew. The police had already found him. He'd been in an accident.

My dad had walked to the A13, waited by the side of the road, and then stepped in front of a lorry.

The police told them that an air ambulance had been called to the scene but wasn't needed. Dad had died almost instantly.

Sometime later, Steve and Grandad returned. Grandad walked in the back door with his head down, hit the table with the palm of his hand, and just said, 'So that's that then.'

Steve followed in a second after and I saw the pain in his eyes. He was emotional but trying to stay strong.

My dad had killed himself.

I broke down.

Tears flooded from my eyes.

I stood hunched over the kitchen counter with my head in my hands. I heard sobbing from my nan, then my mum, and then my brother ...

I clenched my fist, stood up, and punched the top of the kitchen unit.

Why?

Why the fuck has this happened?

Anger and sadness took over me ... my dad, my role model, had gone.

CHAPTER 7

THE FUNERAL

I was running on autopilot. Still trying to get my head around what had happened. Practically, I was busy, helping with funeral arrangements, telling others what had happened, and trying to support Mum with all the admin and press enquiries. But it was all just a distraction from what had happened.

The support we got from others helped. But we still had that question hanging over us: why? My dad was loved by so many people: friends, work colleagues, and clients from his part-time business, and he had a family that loved him. We were bombarded with people sending their condolences. Why didn't he know how loved he was? Why didn't he see it?

Just before the funeral we'd arranged to see Dad in the chapel of rest. They recommended dressing him in clothes he would normally wear, so we chose a casual T-shirt and the beige baggy shorts he always wore. Dad didn't really have that much style; this was his go-to.

Because of how he'd died, we were fearful of how he was going to look, but there wasn't actually a lot of damage to his face. We went in to the chapel of rest together: Mum, Steve, Nan, and Grandad were with me. Seeing his empty body lying there was one of the worst experiences of my life. I kept reminding myself that this was just his body and that my dad lived on, looking over me and guiding me through life. I'm not religious in any way, but I had to hold on to something. I couldn't just accept that he was gone for ever.

They had to raise my dad's chest with metal because it was damaged from the accident. You couldn't see it but it still made him look very fake, like a waxwork; it was hard to see. None of us spent more than a few minutes in there. Steve put in a picture of them doing a walk together and I put in a letter, telling him how much he meant to me and what I was going to do to make him proud. Seeing him like that was something that haunted me for a while. It's hard to think now that it was the last time I saw him physically.

A few days later we gathered at the house ready for the funeral. I'd had a nose bleed half an hour before people started arriving. I had been having a lot of them and they seemed to be triggered by stress. I dreaded what was about to happen. Just the thought of everyone being there was too much; I didn't want people to see me getting upset or talking to me about it. I didn't want to deal with it, I didn't want to talk about it ... I just wanted it to be over.

As we pulled up to the crematorium, we saw that the car park was full. Masses of people were waiting and they turned to face our car as it slowly approached.

Every seat was taken, and people were standing at the back and sides. One of my dad's running friends was standing to my left, looking slightly awkward because he had to stand directly next to us at the front.

We had a pretty small family so the crematorium was almost entirely filled with friends: his running friends, his work friends, his childhood friends. My old football friends he had coached were there and people he knew from refereeing; even his barber was there.

My dad was loved by many but couldn't be helped by any.

That stuck with me. All of those people were there to support him, to give him the send-off he deserved. He was so loved … why couldn't he be helped? Why didn't he feel the love that was now so obvious to see?

I struggled to hold back the tears throughout the funeral. Every time I thought I was managing to keep it together, I turned to see Mum crying and that set me off again. 'Neil's legacy will live on through his two sons, Paul and Steven,' the vicar said. Those words really struck a chord with me; I knew that I now had to do all I could to make Dad proud.

Afterwards we all went to a local bar for the wake. Of course we were mourning but we wanted to make it a real celebration of Dad's life. We put photos of him around the bar – including some funny shots that showed him in happier times: one showing him with his underwear on his head, and a pair of photos with one showing him playing golf as a toddler and another playing golf as an adult. Underneath them it said, *He never did improve at golf!*

As the drinks started to flow, more people started opening up with me about Dad's suicide. At the funeral, nothing had been said about him killing himself. But now, as everyone got more intoxicated, they were more open to talking about it and especially to trying to work out why he did it. I tried to avoid hearing any of those conversations, but a long-time work friend of his broke down in tears as he talked to me about it, with a beer in his hand. I started to drink more too and stayed at the bar with a few of my friends after Mum and the rest of the family went back home.

We all knew Nan was struggling. She'd just lost her only son and she seemed to be giving up on her battle with cancer. She used a wheelchair, unable to really stand, but at least she could eat! Grandad parked her up next to the buffet and just seeing Nan tuck away all of the chicken drumsticks definitely lightened the mood.

The alcohol was a good way to numb the pain. It was also a good way to start talking more openly about Dad and how I felt. As we all got more drunk, it was a way for me to talk more about it all, without feeling judged. But I also used that time to find some normality. I wanted to just be with my friends, at the bar, joking, and doing what we normally would have done. It was a distraction from the thoughts I had going on inside.

When I got home I tried sobering up with a cup of tea and we chatted as a family in the living room. I held it together but when I got into my bedroom I broke. Tears came flooding out like they never had before, and I clenched my fist and stared numbly out of the window. I kept returning to the same question: why has this happened? I cried and cried. I couldn't get the thought that he was really gone out of my mind.

As I sat there in my bedroom, broken, I let go of all of the emotions I had been holding in throughout the day.

Finally, I laid down, closed my eyes, and tried to shut down. I just wanted to shut myself off from everyone. I didn't know how else to deal with it all.

CHAPTER 8

MY LIFE
WITHOUT DAD

As the days went on I found myself trying to be as normal as possible. I carried on like nothing had happened. 'Where are we going tonight then?' I said to one of my friends, a few days after we'd laid Dad to rest. To me, the funeral signalled the end of the grieving process.

Keeping busy was the only way to take my mind off things. When I was busy, I didn't have to think, I didn't get emotional. So that became my default coping mechanism. That's why I decided to go clubbing a week after it happened.

I'll never forget the surprised looks of the people who knew about Dad, when they saw me out. An old friend from college said, 'Are you okay? I didn't expect to see you ...' 'I'm fine,' I told him. 'I just want to have some fun.' Inside I wasn't fine. Inside I hurt. But I knew that carrying on as normal and showing people that I was okay would stop anyone else talking about it.

When I was alone and thinking about Dad, I'd get upset. I had always been quite sensitive and wasn't afraid to show my emotions. At times I'd speak to Mum, but I always felt like I didn't want to burden her with everything; after all, she was going through it too.

Just over a month after Dad died, my nan lost her battle with cancer. Grandad lost his only son and his wife of over 50 years within the space of a month.

Being the old, stubborn gent that he is, he never showed much emotion, but I knew that this was the worst thing he'd ever experienced. Nan had always been tough. She'd been diagnosed with cancer and given just six months to live, but with treatment and a really strong mentality (not to mention a strong husband) she managed to survive longer than expected. But after Dad's first accident and all the visits to the mental health unit, it had just gone on getting harder. And then she had to experience something much worse. After Dad died, Nan just gave up. After Dad's funeral, when she said her last goodbye, she just didn't want to live any more.

Nan's funeral was a smaller affair but a good way to pay our respects to an amazing woman. I loved my nan dearly but I struggled to express that emotion at her funeral. I did cry, but it was thinking about saying goodbye to Dad at the same place, just over a month before, that made the tears come.

Being such a close-knit family, it was heartbreaking losing two such special people within such a short space of time. But with two funerals over, life had to go on. I was keen to get back to "normality" as soon as possible. I felt like work would just be another way to keep busy, another way to carry on life without Dad.

But the people at work told me to take as much time off as possible. And because of everything I'd been dealing with, my doctor signed me off work for a month. There were some great guys at work, but I'd been really struggling to enjoy my job for a while, and I was afraid that people would judge me or my dad, or simply see me in a different way.

I knew I had some tough decisions to make. I'd been studying network systems before Dad died, and I knew that if I got the qualifications I'd get promoted and earn more money.

Unfortunately, they were the only reasons I was doing it. So, with work and study on hold, I took the time to think about what sort of future I really wanted ...

When it came, going back to work was tough. Being at work was okay, but getting there involved a 50-minute drive, and getting home took at least an hour. Most of the way, there and back, I would listen to the music that Dad and I had shared, and I would cry. I remembered texting him two days before he died, recommending he check out Jason Mraz. We liked lots of similar music and I knew he'd love his music too. He never did listen to the album, so I found myself playing it on repeat while I commuted into work, thinking of Dad, knowing that I'd never see him again.

When I got back to work I expected people to talk about what had happened. Obviously my supervisor and manager knew what had happened, and in fact, my supervisor was very supportive throughout Dad's first accident and all the battles afterwards. But my fear of what people would say was short-lived. No one said anything. It was a male-dominated office – 50 men and just two women. 'Oh, you're back,' one of the lads in the office said, 'where've you been?' The question threw me. I had guessed that people would have been told. 'Ah, my dad died ...' I said. 'Shit!' he said in response. He felt embarrassed. He apologised and walked off, but not before patting me on the shoulder. No one else said anything and I certainly wasn't going to tell anyone how he had died.

I stayed at work for just over a month. I could still see myself progressing in the company and making more money, but I just wasn't happy. I had started to hate those five days at work every week and was living for the weekends. I couldn't face the thought of repeating that pattern over and over again.

And then it hit me ...

Dad had been through this too. He had worked a 9–5 job for his whole life, one that he didn't really enjoy that much but kept on doing because it paid well. He worked, worked, and worked, saving up the money he was earning for an early retirement. He had been holding out for the day he could enjoy life and do all the things he'd always wanted to do. But he never got there.

Fuck. What am I doing?

Why am I still here?

'Follow your heart and not your head,' Dad had always told me.

After talking it through with Mum, I decided to leave work. Again, the company was really supportive of my decision. Honestly, I had no idea what I was going to do for money. All I knew was that I would do anything in my power to live by my rules – to find a job that I loved and to create more freedom around what I did.

I played with the idea of going to university to become a PE teacher. I'd always enjoyed PE at school and admired some of the PE teachers. I could even see myself teaching others. When I say I played with the idea, I did actually get accepted by two universities and did two weeks of work experience at my old school. Looking back I was very close to going but I wasn't ready to leave home, and the urge to start my own business was a lot stronger than the thought of going to university.

I put more of my focus on selling on eBay and started to increase the amount of money I was making. I'd reinvest some of it into new products but I wasted a lot on going out, drinking alcohol, and buying fancy shit.

After a little while, Dad's inheritance money went to Mum. She had never really had a lot of money for herself, and whatever money she did have, she had always spent it on me and Steve.

I'd just turned 19, Steve was 21, but Mum treated us like mature adults. She trusted us and wanted to give us both an opportunity to use that money for ourselves. So she gave us each a good share. Dad had worked hard all his life. He certainly hadn't been rich but he had saved his money wisely.

I wanted to use the money to make him proud. But as time went on, the thought of having that money started to feel like a weight around my neck. Dad could have spent it on anything he'd wanted, but he had saved so hard, for all of us. It almost felt like dirty money at times – money that should have secured his happy retirement – and every time I spent it on something stupid, I hated myself for it.

I knew there was a ceiling on how much I could make on eBay, so the inheritance money gave me a different opportunity. It allowed me to invest in an online business of my own, selling men's clothing accessories. I put most of the inheritance money towards buying stock, getting a website made, branding, and investing in online courses that taught me the basics of running an online business.

Mum was so supportive of my decision. She just wanted what was best for me and knew that eventually I'd figure things out. (Even though she found it hard explaining to her friends what I was actually doing for a career.) I wondered if Dad would have done the same as me, but he was far more black and white about life – with the mentality that you should study, go to work, save money, and retire.

The dream of creating an online business that would essentially lead to freedom from the 9–5 became my everything. Every hour that passed I'd be doing some form of work, writing down ideas or browsing the internet looking for ways to learn more. Being able to make money from my laptop without actually going to work and having the ability to work whenever and wherever was a huge motivator for me. What 19-year-old lad wouldn't want to make a ton of money, sitting on a white sandy beach with his laptop, drinking a cold bottled beer?

Starting this business became my everything. It kept me busy and distracted me from dealing with Dad's suicide. But I didn't just invest that money wisely on the business, I also went out and spent it on materialistic items, things to boost my status.

At 19, I wanted to look good. I wanted to show people that I ran my own business. My ego was driving me to chase an evermore luxurious lifestyle.

It started small – buying branded T-shirts for £45, when I had always just bought two for £10. Then there was the car: a Ford Focus Zetec S with three doors and tinted windows. It had all the bells and whistles, the sporty rims, the Bluetooth connection (quite a new thing at the time), and a really loud sound system. I got it on finance as I couldn't afford to pay for it outright, but I didn't care. I had gone from a Renault Clio, where I paid more insurance than the car was actually worth, to a brand new Ford Focus.

What will my friends say?

How cool am I going to look when I turn up in this?

The car felt good for a while; it numbed the pain. But only for a short while. It wasn't long before I was pretty bored of it. And it definitely didn't make me feel as good as I thought it would. Nothing did.

I *could* see a life without Dad, I *could* see a future. But I thought it would only work if I kept life exciting: working, spending, clubbing, drinking, driving, dating ...

I thought if I blocked Dad out, and if I kept myself distracted and busy, I'd be able to deal with it.

I was wrong ...

CHAPTER 9

A KNIFE TO
MY CHEST

I was at the lowest point I'd ever been.

I was lost.

I was confused.

I was hurt.

But I wasn't showing it. I was still hiding behind the mask that hid all of my emotions. All of my shame, guilt, and pain were safely hidden behind the masks I wore for work, friends, and family.

Inside I was hurting but the mask just made people think I was somehow dealing with the fact my dad had just killed himself. I wasn't just trying to fool everyone else – I was also trying to fool myself. I'd hit rock bottom. I didn't know how to deal with it, and the pain was getting more intense with every negative thought and action I had.

I can remember some of the thoughts that went through my head ...

I can't handle not seeing Dad again; I need to see him.

Why did he do it? Why did he leave us behind?

I'm just like my dad; people used to compare us ... will I go the same way as him?

I never want to get married or have kids, my dad won't be there ...

I can't carry on like this ...

I remember on a few occasions, I did actually think about doing it ...

Lying in bed one night, I found myself curled up with my head in a pillow. Memories of Dad came flooding back.

I'm in the same situation as he was.

That memory and that thought triggered something in me. I got up, walked downstairs, grabbed a knife, and held it to my chest. My breathing raced and tears streamed down my face.

Everyone was asleep. No one knew what I was going through because I'd been faking happiness. Was this how he had felt?

I don't think I could ever have known what he had gone through. I do know that the thoughts I had were not strong enough to make me take my own life that night. But I'd hit the black hole of depression and didn't know how to deal with it.

Maybe I'd just wanted to try and feel like Dad; maybe I'd wanted to try and see his decision through his eyes ...

Why did my dad take his own life?

Why couldn't he turn to one of his many friends and family members who loved him dearly?

On paper he had everything.

He held down his two jobs, which meant he was well paid. He had a loving wife, two sons, and supportive parents. He kept active by running daily and he became the National Veteran Champion at 1,500m in his early 40s.

So with a supportive network of friends and family, with financial security and full health, why did he feel like suicide was the only option?

That question haunted me for years after we lost him. And trying to answer that question led me to feelings of guilt, blame, and a sense of abandonment.

Did I do something wrong?

Did he not love me enough to stay?

Should I have handled his depression differently?

Should I have said something differently?

Why couldn't I give him a reason to not do what he did?

I think everyone goes through these feelings after they lose someone to suicide. But they took me over and led me to a very dark place.

What did I have to live for?

I remember driving home late one night with tears streaming down my face. There were no cars on the road and I felt, very strongly, that I didn't want to be alive any more.

All I could focus on was the overriding thought that I just wanted to see him again. For days on end I cried endless streams of tears, begging for him to come back, begging to see him just one more time. To hold him, to run with him, to make him laugh, to hear him say he was proud of me.

At that moment, driving in my car through the town I grew up in, the thought that I would never see him again was just too hard to handle. Maybe the only way for me to see him again ... was to join him. My arms straightened as I held the wheel with both hands as I approached a sharp bend. What if I swerved here? What if I sped up? What if I ended the emotional pain right now?

To the side of the bend, there was a big building. All I had to do was drive straight into it ... I was just 50m from the bend. With my eyes closed, tears making them heavy, I held my breath. I had seconds to talk myself out of it. Maybe only seconds left to live.

I opened my eyes, let out the breath I was holding, and sharply steered right. What the hell was I doing? Why was I being so stupid? I couldn't inflict more pain on Mum, on Steve, on the people around me. I still had things to live for.

That might have snapped me out of it, but it didn't. There were more times like this as the months went by. I kept coming back to the same thought, over and over again: *should I end this?*

The depressive state I was in at just 19, with my whole life ahead of me, was scary. It's one I wouldn't wish on anyone and one I never want to go back to.

I didn't feel like myself in any of those moments. I felt like I was being controlled by something other than me. I think I was trying to answer that question of why my dad did it. How could he do it? Maybe I'd been putting myself into those situations to see if I could recreate the feelings, the emotions, and the pain he must have faced when he decided he had nothing to live for.

But for me, at the vital moment, I always found a glimpse of hope from somewhere. And over all the years of sadness that followed, and the self-realisation too, I overcame the pain, I overcame the feelings of guilt, and most importantly ... I forgave him.

I could understand ...

I could almost understand how he might have felt so desperate to kill himself.

I used to think suicide was selfish. Heck, I even said so earlier.

But suicide isn't selfish ...

I've seen why suicide can feel like not just a choice, but the only choice. I'm sure that's what Dad must have felt. He had family, friends, money, safety, his parents. He had so many "reasons" why he shouldn't do it, but he still did it.

The pain he went through after his breakdown and from the deep depression he must have been feeling was obviously far greater than any reason he had to stay with us.

His perception of life had collapsed and darkened, and he must have felt as if he'd lost all choice in life.

When your perception of life is intact, you look to the future and you get excited about what's about to happen. When it collapses, you can't see past the darkness. You don't think about tomorrow, about next year, or your potential future. All you see is the moment you're in right now, the depression you feel, and the struggle of getting out of it.

I think this collapsed perception of life is key. Because when your perception of life collapses, you lose control of everything.

You lose control of your relationships, your career and money, your family, and everything you've tried to control in your life. You lose control of yourself and your thoughts, and that's when depression takes over.

When this happens, when you lose control of everything, you're simply left with a feeling of nothingness. You're empty. Nothing matters any more ... you don't matter any more.

With your perception of life in tatters, it feels like all control has gone.

But there's one thing you still control, one all-important decision you can still make.

Do I end this pain, or fight it for another day?

I'm sure that's how my dad felt.

Ironically, I think that suicidal ideation finally gives back that feeling of being in control – and that can make a person feel complete. Even if someone has not felt in control of any other situation in their life, this situation – right here, right now – on the brink of taking their own life, is their decision, it's them in control.

Imagine you've been sent to prison, knowing you'll be locked away for decades. Imagine staring at the same four walls for most of the rest of your life and imagine how easily your perception of life might collapse as a result. Imagine the despair you'd feel, and the loss of hope. I'm sure you can see why there is such a high suicide rate in prison. Even when prisoners are released, this collapsed view of life can endure.

Why would someone want to live if they have no hope? If they see nothing but darkness?

People struggle to understand the pain people must be experiencing for them to make that decision. I sure did. But now I know that when your perception of life collapses, the pain of living becomes unbearable.

After listening to numerous people who have survived suicide attempts, and reflecting on my dad's suicide, most of them talked about just wanting the pain to end. Of wanting it to stop hurting.

Death is physically painful but the emotional pain people experience in making that decision is far greater than the physical pain they'll endure.

Something I've never really shared before stands out to me here ...

When my dad decided to walk in front of a lorry, the reports from witnesses say that after the collision, he smiled. He lay there, on the road, his life seconds away from ending, and he smiled.

I've battled with this for years. Why did my dad smile when it happened? Surely he'd be happier alive with us right now? What did I do wrong that made death seem better than spending time with me?

But reflecting on it now, I feel a sense of ease, it helps me let go ...

My dad was in terrible pain, a pain far greater than getting hit by a 40-ton lorry driving at 50mph. The physical pain he endured from colliding with that lorry took away the far greater pain of his deep depression.

He had already known the physical pain an accident like this would inflict due to his first suicide attempt. But even after six months of care and medication, support from family and friends, and, on some level, knowing the endless reasons why he shouldn't ... he was still in unbearable pain.

That one decision, that one choice that played over and over again in his head every day, was too much to handle. He said 'no' to it over and over again, he tried fighting it, but in the end he just couldn't fight it any more.

My dad was in the best physical shape a guy in his mid-40s could be in when he died, but he never got the support he needed for his mental health. We weren't given a manual on how to deal with it, and neither was he.

If he'd have broken his leg, he'd have been sent home in a cast. We'd have known how we needed to support him. And he would have known when he could get back to walking, back to running, and back to full recovery. We'd all have known what medication he needed and when he should take it.

When my dad had a breakdown, we had no instructions and no manual to help us understand how to support him. So we took him to the doctors who prescribed some antidepressants, and then he was sent home.

But that didn't help us and maybe it hasn't helped someone you know ... so where do we go from here?

What do we say? What do we do?

It isn't just more support that we need, it's more acknowledgment. We need to talk about these issues and how they affect us. And we need to start talking about suicide as a health issue.

How many times have you had a physical exam – blood tests, blood pressure tests, etc. There are plenty of tests to check for illness within our body, but how often is our mental health checked as part of a routine health assessment?

Suicide is a subject that people just don't talk about. People are inevitably frightened to admit the times they've felt suicidal, and this silence is a huge factor behind the shocking statistics right around the world.

It's time we spoke up. It's time we let ourselves open up about our feelings.

CHAPTER 10

FEELING F.I.N.E.

It was time to focus on myself.

My doctor referred me to a counsellor, who helped me understand depression in a different way. I found that simply admitting my depression, and opening up to someone, helped me deal with the thoughts, feelings, and emotions that had been holding me in that dark hole of depression.

The release was uplifting – I started to see light instead of complete darkness. I'd only been to two counselling sessions and being able to talk about it really did help. But I stopped going after that. I felt like I didn't need it; I'd done what I'd been advised I should do.

As the months passed, I dealt with things more openly and started to invest more time into my own personal growth. I was reading self-help books and carried on working hard on my business. I'd also started going out with Amy – now my wife – and that helped me in so many ways.

But I knew that I still had to learn how to help myself too.

I had begun the process of openly talking about some of the emotions that held me in that dark place. I felt like I was slowly starting to get back to "normal" life. But deep down, I was still suffering. I had lost my dad to suicide and no amount of talking was going to make me feel better just like that.

I worked more, went out more, drank more, and spent the majority of my earnings on clothes, my car, nights out, and the growing stack of self-help books. But I was still fooling myself. I thought that returning to "normal" life and doing the things a "normal" person would do was me being okay.

It wasn't.

I was merely using distractions to keep me away from the deeper emotions I still hadn't opened up to or dealt with. And I was feeling it. Not just emotionally, but physically too.

I was more vocal and open to people close to me, but whenever the conversation about my dad came up with anyone else, I'd lie. It wasn't that I was ashamed to talk about it, I just feared the judgement. If I told someone my dad took his own life, surely they'd judge him, me, and my family? It would also make the conversation awkward and I didn't want that. So whenever someone asked how my dad died, I'd always say, 'In a road accident.' I'd never tell them it was suicide.

One evening at Amy's house I was complaining about the back pain I'd been having. Dad had been a trained physiotherapist and a few years ago he'd have been able to help me. But there I was, still struggling with Dad no longer there to help. Amy told me, 'You should get Ann's number, she's a masseuse.' At first it sounded like a good idea, especially as she was far cheaper than others I'd tried. But then she said something that got my attention, 'She's quite weird though – a bit like a witch! She seems to know stuff about people.'

All I wanted was a massage to help ease my back pain and Amy had given me a "witch's" number? I booked up, scared but intrigued.

Not knowing what to expect, I walked into the "witch's" house. She went by the surprisingly conventional name of Ann, and she lived in a very cosy house, overflowing with candles, ornaments, books, and tarot cards.

We walked into the room nearest the front door. It was dark. The curtains were closed and she had a stool for me to sit down on and a couch for the massage. 'Take your oils,' she said, pointing to the cabinet to my left.

It was like she thought I knew what I was doing, like she had confused me with someone else. I approached the cabinet and was about to ask how many oils when she said softly, 'Take just three oils.'

We talked a little bit about a mutual friend and then I told her the reason I'd gone to see her. I told her about my back pain and asked for her advice. I got on the couch and she went ahead with the massage; it wasn't a typical sports massage like I was expecting. In the dim light, with soft music playing in the background, a dim light on, and with Ann not applying too much pressure, it was relaxing.

I lay in silence throughout most of the massage. At the end, she identified a key problem with my back and recommended a chiropractor. Leaving her house, I was intrigued to discover more. There was something about her, her energy ...

I returned a week later, chose my oils, and sat down. I placed the oils gently on the couch, waiting for Ann to enter the room. I'd had a pretty tough week with work and I was looking forward to a really relaxing massage.

Ann took her seat opposite me and said, 'How are you?'

'Fine,' I replied.

She chuckled. 'Do you know what fine really means?'

'No,' I replied.

'Fucked up, Insecure, Neurotic, and Emotional. Now tell me why you're really here ...

Her words pierced me, I really didn't know what to say. This small lady in her late 60s, who was supposed to be a witch, with her long, curly, grey hair, and her long dress and multiple bracelets on each arm had just said "fuck". My natural instinct was to laugh.

She sat in silence. Her failure to laugh back made me feel awkward. 'I'm here for my back,' I replied.

'No you're not,' she said.

I laughed again, debating whether or not I should have come. I could have just got up and left. Ann looked straight at me but the prolonged eye contact didn't make me feel uncomfortable.

'I lost my dad to suicide two years ago,' I said softly, looking at the floor.

She'd broken me. She had grabbed the knife, chopped it straight through the onion, and now she was ready to start peeling back the layers …

'How does that make you feel?' she asked.

The word "feel" hit me hard and I had to look inside.

'I feel like I'm dealing with it well,' I said.

Consciously I was telling the truth, I was dealing with it, but subconsciously I wasn't so sure. It was almost like Ann could see through the bravado. She challenged me again: 'What made you come here?'

'My back pain,' I said again.

But deep down, I knew Ann wasn't going to be the one to cure my back pain. I had been drawn to her because of the words "weird", "witch", and "psychic". And she knew it.

'I think you're here for other reasons,' she told me.

She got me to talk, to open up, and even though I held back at first, she got through to me. At times, the tears streamed down my face. I started to see the things I was doing wrong.

I was working too hard, doing too much, and distracting myself from the underlying emotions I wasn't dealing with.

She made me understand my dad's decision more, and I felt connected to him, through her.

The massage after our talk was more relaxing than before. I felt a sense of freedom, my muscles felt more relaxed, and thoughts raced through my mind as I lay on the couch.

Afterwards, I sat in my car, crying, reliving the moments around Dad's death. I didn't know if they were "bad" tears. Was I depressed? I remember Ann telling me that it was natural to cry; it was better to let go of the pain than try to hold it in.

Even though, on the surface, I was more upset than I had been going in, I felt different. Stronger. Things she had said to me kept reappearing in my thoughts, and at times, I could feel my tears turning to a small smile or a chuckle. I was more excited for my future. It felt as if the healing had begun.

With each week came more self-reflection; Ann continued to peel back the layers. We talked about the concept of the ego and Ann suggested that perhaps my ego was helping to protect me from my low self-esteem.

As the months went by, I started to feel different.

Sure, there were some evenings I'd cancel, and some evenings I really didn't feel like going. Sometimes facing the fear and knowing that you're going to discuss all the shit you've got going on is hard to face. But it's well worth it when you do.

There was nothing abnormal about Ann. I don't think she possessed psychic abilities or was connected to my dad in any way. She doesn't claim to be a witch, a psychic, or a medium ... she's just Ann. She's a remarkable woman with a challenging past who overcame it and loves helping others. She was the person I felt good opening up to.

I felt as if I was becoming a better version of myself, someone I thought I never could be. I stopped trying to hide from my emotions. I didn't run away from the grief.

I think I was drawn to Ann being "weird" because I wanted answers. I wanted to find out what had really happened to my dad. The counselling I'd had before had always felt quite forced, almost like I had to think and talk. But with Ann, it was a slower, gentler process, and to begin with it was more about the massage. I had no expectations, but the day I managed to open up to her was when I started feeling better. Feeling like I could live a life ... without Dad.

I still see Ann today, typically once a month or once every two weeks. Why? Because it's good to talk.

That first day when I walked into Ann's, I had perfected the art of putting on a good front.

I'd spent two years trying to show my strength, doing everything a typical young adult would do. I worked as much as I possibly could, just to distract myself from having to deal with my feelings. It wasn't conscious. I had just gone straight into "man up" mode. But through speaking about the issues I was facing and the way I was feeling, I learnt to deal with them. The feelings I was having were normal. I was normal.

The effects of opening up were amazing. It helped me turn my life around. I felt like I could start to handle what had happened to my dad. It helped my relationship with my family and partner become stronger. My business started to improve, and I started to grow and take on more opportunities. Learning to open up really helped.

But getting better was never just about opening up and everything becoming "normal". Opening up to someone is only ever the start of it. I spent weeks, months, and eventually years diving deeper into who I am. I started to understand myself, I started to understand my dad's suicide, and I forgave him as well as myself. Ann gave me book after book, she got me to think deeper with every session, and I started to discover what made me happy – not what kept my ego happy but what truly made me happy.

When we open up for the first time, it's a dangerous place to be. The wounds we've ignored for years are now open, the bandages are off. But being able to understand, forgive, and eventually become comfortable with who we are is a process that doesn't happen overnight.

Burying how you feel and using short-term distractions is the most damaging thing you can do. Opening up, understanding, and forgiving is the best thing you can do.

I know that if the feelings resurface, none of the old short-term distractions will help. But looking after my mental health, understanding myself and others, and forgiving where I need to forgive, these things will all help me. I know that the secret, hard though it may be, is to understand and forgive.

When you open up for the first time talking about things becomes easier. It's like anything – the fear attached to being vulnerable will always try to stop you. But facing that fear and doing it will help you deal with things more openly, so you can handle things better.

We hear a lot about what it means to be a "real man". To me, a real man isn't afraid to talk about his thoughts and feelings. (And I know that if anyone laughs about that or thinks I'm weak for it, they've got more underlying issues than I have!) If someone can't accept that you need to open up about how you feel, maybe they're not someone you need in your life.

A real man understands. A real man is sufficiently self-aware to know how they feel and are able to deal with it openly when times get tough.

A real man isn't afraid of vulnerability.

Opening up doesn't have to involve a one-to-one counselling session. Everyone is different. You might want to write it down, or talk to a family member, friend, or colleague. Don't be afraid to try multiple therapists. Everyone is different. Everyone deals with things differently. But holding onto your emotional pain and burying it doesn't help anyone.

CHAPTER 11

WE'RE ALL FIGHTING OUR OWN BATTLES

As time went on, the normality of life did make it harder to grieve. Life almost became a distraction from dealing with the pain I felt from Dad's suicide.

As a family, we stuck together. In some ways, Dad's suicide had brought us closer. Dad was very distant as he battled his depression and those last few months were like a dress rehearsal for life as a family of three.

But with life moving on, the conversations about Dad's suicide and how we felt individually just stopped. I always knew I could talk to Mum. I'd always been open with her in the past, but I knew she was trying to deal with it all in her own way and I didn't want to burden her. It was also the same with Steve. We were close as brothers but we didn't really talk much about Dad's suicide and how it affected us. Maybe we all felt like we had to battle on alone, just so we didn't burden one another.

In the immediate aftermath of a death, things are different. You get floods of support at the beginning. And while you're trying to come to terms with what's happened, you're also distracted by funeral arrangements and the legal stuff. But once that's all over … that's when it really hits you. It hits you like a ton of bricks. You try to put on a brave face to show you're okay, but that's when the loneliness is really brutal.

I felt like my loneliness would tear me apart. The battle I had in trying to deal with Dad's suicide – and what it meant to me personally – while life went back to "normal", was something I'd never wish on anyone. But I wasn't the only one battling that loneliness …

Mum was struggling too. She had always been such a hands-on Mum, and had done everything for me and Steve. We were her world. But as we had grown more independent, I felt as if Mum started to lose that sense of purpose. Looking back, I'm sure she felt under-appreciated too. Every day she'd make us breakfast, make Dad's lunch for work, she'd do the housework, cook dinner, taxi us round to all our sports events, and I don't think any of us showed her any appreciation for it. We just came to expect it from her. That was Mum.

We had it easy. And because Dad didn't do much around the house, it almost sent that message that, as men, that was an acceptable way to behave. Mum would dish up dinner and we'd guzzle it down, thank her, and leave it all for her to clear up. Dad would often do the same before seeing his physiotherapy patients in the evenings. He was used to having everything ready for him before he left for work in the day, and he had everything done for him when he got home.

Mum's life was getting lonelier. Sometimes she would have a drink by herself – just a glass of wine. Just a drink in the evening when Dad was working. Just something to help fill the time. And then, one glass had turned into two glasses …

Throughout Dad's depression and after his suicide, Mum didn't drink. I think she was purely running on autopilot, taking everything as it came, and not wanting to inflict any more pain on her boys. But after everything that had happened, and as life started going back to "normal", she started to drink again.

At the time, I couldn't get my head around it. Why couldn't she just stop? But I guess it was her only method of dealing with the grief. I guess it was just the only tool she had to numb the pain. While I was putting on a front, chasing short-term pleasures, and crying quietly in my room at night, and while Steve was very quiet and focusing on university, Mum was drinking. We were all dealing with the grief and we were all dealing with our other personal battles, but we were all dealing with them differently.

In December 2010, 20 months after Dad died, Mum was taken into hospital. The alcohol addiction was now affecting her physically too. She was jaundiced, she was having fits, and her liver scan results were really worrying.

Just seeing Mum in hospital was a huge shock. Mum was the rock that kept us together as a family, she was the one who kept us both going after Dad's suicide ... we couldn't lose her as well.

I was numb. On the day they admitted her, Steve and I drove back from the hospital in silence. We just didn't know what to say any more. We couldn't accept this was happening.

But Mum was strong. She pulled through and came out of hospital a different person to the one who had gone in. She was our mum again. Physically, she looked healthier. Mentally, she seemed stronger. It was such a relief to get our mum back. The thought of losing her had almost been too much to handle; I'm not sure I would have been able to cope.

As always, we expected Mum to just carry on. No matter what was happening in our lives, we expected her to be able to rise above it all. Shortly after being released from hospital, she cooked dinner for nine people.

Mum worked so hard to stay sober but the instinct to drink seemed too deep-rooted. How else could she escape the pain? It was such a heart-wrenching feeling when you'd smell alcohol on her breath or find a bottle hidden away. I just felt sorry for her. Mum was broken. She ended up in hospital again but her strength carried her through again. There was a fight in her I'd never seen before.

I had never quite been able to understand Mum's battles with alcohol – why would someone as loving as her "choose" to drink? The immediate judgement of someone who self-sabotages through an addiction is that they're weak, that they're giving up. But after seeing Dad's breakdown happening, and after dealing with his depression and suicide, I saw just how strong my mum had been through all those years. She had been battling demons for longer than I could ever imagine. She had lived with emotional trauma that most of us would have struggled to deal with.

No matter how hard she fought, she kept falling back to drink, and it seemed like she was running out of options. I knew Mum wanted to stop and she had tried so many things – AA meetings, hypnotherapy, counselling, a home detox, and even tablets that made her vomit if she drank. She had tried going cold turkey and in desperation she had given me her purse and car keys so she couldn't buy any alcohol. But none of it had worked.

I wanted to try something completely different. One afternoon, when Mum was struggling, I took her to see Ann. Once I'd convinced her to go once, she went again and again ...

And then it happened ... Ann didn't get her to deal with the addiction. Ann got her to deal with the cause – all the emotional pain that she'd bottled up and numbed with alcohol. After seeing Dad break down and take his own life, after seeing other patients in the mental health unit struggling with their own addictions (and discovering more about myself and how I reacted), I started to see how addiction could be a way of distracting ourselves from emotional pain we don't want to deal with. Addiction is that short-term fix – it's a way to numb those emotions. Dad was addicted to work and to making money, and those things distracted him from the emotional trauma he didn't want to deal with. When Dad died, I too became addicted to work, and addicted to spending money as a way of distracting myself and numbing the grief from Dad's suicide.

The change in Mum was so noticeable. More and more days passed when she didn't drink at all. And she seemed happier than I had seen her for a very long time. With every day she went sober and with every self-help book she read, she seemed to be improving.

Mum hasn't touched a drop of alcohol since. Her doctors were amazed – the physical damage she had done to her liver disappeared faster than they had ever seen before. And that was just the start. Mum studied and became a counsellor, and that has played a huge part in helping me deal with Dad's suicide too.

Honestly, it's hard writing this. Trying to save someone you love from an addiction and seeing them slowly get worse without any control over them is hard. But I think the truth is that being the addict is harder.

I know my mum's recovery is a sign that things can get better. Even when it feels like you've tried every possible solution, please keep trying.

CHAPTER 12

NAPPY DUTY!

I think I want to be a dad! The thought had been playing on my mind for a few weeks, and then suddenly, one day, the force of it really shook me. It was a few months after Dad died, and maybe I thought that by becoming a dad, I'd be able to grieve better, or I'd be able to forget about Dad not being in my life anymore. Or maybe it was my way of trying to let his memory live on, by becoming a Dad myself. Back then, it definitely wasn't the right time. And those thoughts didn't occupy my mind for long.

But fast forward a year and I was dating Amy ... We used to talk about the different lives we'd led before we'd met. I had been dealing with Dad's depression while she was dealing with pregnancy. I had been grieving over Dad's suicide while she was giving birth and raising her son, Freddie, from a previous relationship.

When we first started dating, it was casual. I knew she had a child and neither of us were looking for anything serious at the time. We got on really well, we shared a lot of similar interests, and I loved her independence and maturity. I really admired the way she'd handled becoming a mum at 19. Deep down, I think I craved that maturity and stability. I was all over the place; it was what I needed in my life.

I remember the first time the subject came up. We were enjoying a film and a takeaway, and she asked, 'Do you live with your mum and dad?' I was shocked at first. I'd just imagined she already knew about my dad. Surely one of our mutual friends would have told her? 'My dad's dead,' I replied bluntly. I could see how uncomfortable my reply made her feel and she apologised straight away. I quickly moved the conversation onto something else. I would do everything I could not to talk about Dad's death at that time.

We continued dating for a few months and she even paid for our first holiday away together. We'd spoken about Freddie and I'd ask her about him, but I hadn't met him properly. I was a little scared of meeting him and she was protective of him. She wanted to make sure our relationship was strong enough before introducing me into his life. Freddie still had his own dad in his life and was seeing him every weekend at the time.

Eventually, I met Freddie just before his second birthday and as time went on, our bond grew closer. I still lived at home with Mum, and it took me a while to commit everything to the relationship and my role as a stepdad. I worried about what people would think of me becoming a stepdad in my early 20s, and because I was such a mummy's boy I kept putting off the decision to commit deeper. Admittedly, the washing, cleaning, and cooking services Mum provided were hard to step away from!

It must've been hard for Amy though. We'd spend a weekend together as a family, doing what most young families would do, and then I'd go back to Mum's and not see them both for a few days. That must have been hard for Freddie too.

But it was obvious that Amy and Freddie were bringing out the best in me. I was learning so much about myself every time I was with them. And as time went on, I started to commit more to the role of being a boyfriend and a stepdad. I might not have been ready to call myself that back then, but I was starting to play more of a role in Freddie's life. One thing was certain though, I wasn't going to change a stinky nappy! I made it clear to Amy that nappy duty was hers. I just couldn't get my head round the thought of dealing with a toddler's poo. Maybe that was my ego kicking in again, maybe it was the fear of doing it wrong, or just the fact it was, well, poo. Inevitably, it wasn't long before Freddie did the deed while I was babysitting him for a few hours and I had no one else to turn to. I dropped my stubbornness and got stuck in. Yuck.

Around 1,502 Freddie nappies later, I'm glad I got a lot more hands-on. I wanted to be a dad who was always there, a dad who was confident in being a parent, and also, hopefully, a role model. He's thrown up on my shoulder and I haven't minded. We've watched endless hours of *Thomas the Tank Engine* together and I've enjoyed it almost as much as him. I was there for his first school day and parents' evening. I helped him learn to ride a bike. I've been there to see him smile and throw tantrums. Experiencing all of that and being there to see him grow up has given so much more meaning to my life.

By having Freddie in my life, I saw that the role of a father wasn't just about me and my issues. It wasn't just about my ego, worries, and insecurities. My life became much bigger than that. My heart had grown bigger.

Amy had brought out the best in me. I adored her as a girlfriend and a mum. The two of them gave me more hope and more things to wake up for every morning. I had more reasons to become the best Paul I could be, so that I could support them.

Writing this now, I think I really underestimated just how much they did for me. That time spent with Amy at the beginning, when I was really getting to know her, was so valuable. She helped keep me grounded at a time when I really needed it. Then meeting Freddie and playing a more active role in his life as time went on gave me even more reasons to think outside myself.

I still regret being very hesitant with Freddie at the start – and not really understanding how my role as a dad must have impacted on him growing up. One minute I was there, I was a father figure to him, and then I was out clubbing, or back at my other home for a few days. There was also a time when the relationship ended. I was 23, confused, and not sure what I wanted. I wasn't "all in", and I decided I wanted to travel. We split up and I travelled to Thailand for six weeks with my best friend. While I was gone, I distanced myself from speaking to them. I couldn't bring myself to do it and I felt guilty for doing what I'd done.

Even after I returned, I planned to go back to Thailand again, but on my own. I spoke to Amy one evening and she mentioned that Freddie really wanted to see me. She didn't put any pressure on me, but asked if I wanted to go to the park with him after school. At first, I wasn't sure, but I did want to make sure he was okay. I couldn't imagine never seeing him again, and I couldn't imagine myself not seeing Amy again. So I said I'd meet Amy and we'd collect him from school together.

When I saw Amy, my heart raced. I had a rush of all those feelings I'd had when we'd started dating. We walked to school together and waited at the gate for Freddie to come out. I'd bought him a stuffed monkey as a toy, ready to tell him I'd captured it from Thailand, but as soon as he saw me, he ran towards me, arms wide, and gave me the tightest hug he'd ever given me. 'Paul, Paul, Paul, Daddy Paul,' he kept saying over and over again.

We went to the park and flew his kite, and I caught up with Amy. It felt good. It felt right. On the way home, my head was spinning. Fuck. What had I done?

Seeing them again almost made me feel like I'd been living a fake life without them ... the travelling, the clubbing, the freedom to sleep whenever I wanted, and drink 50% vodka from a bucket was fun ... but it wasn't fulfilling. And I could see it for what it was – another example of me chasing short-term pleasure to distract myself from how I was really feeling inside.

I wanted them. I needed them. We met up again a few days later and went out for dinner together. At the time I didn't want to tell Amy, I didn't want to make a rash decision or just tell her straight up that I wanted them back. I had to earn it and try to show her how I truly felt. I'd messed her around enough. The time for saying all the right things was past, it was time to show her I meant what I said.

But there was a problem. Amy had just started dating someone else. She'd waited to hear from me for months and I'd ignored her. It hadn't got serious yet, but for my ego it meant I wasn't just competing with my sense of guilt, shame, and sadness; I was competing with another man! I knew I'd have to show Amy how much she meant to me, so I started planning more thoughtful dates for the two of us. I wrote her a long letter, acknowledging the mistakes I'd made and telling her just how much she and Freddie made me feel.

When we met up, I made the sorts of promises to her that I'd never made to anyone else. And when I got emotional while I was talking to her, I let it happen. I'd fucked up, we all knew it, and I needed them both back in my life.

We decided to give it another go and this time I felt a lot more settled. I had tried walking the grass on the other side of the road, without realising that I already had everything I wanted.

We went on a three-week "flashpacking" trip around Europe (basically flying and staying in hotels). The three of us went from Barcelona to Monaco, Monaco to Genoa, Genoa to Milan, and Milan to Paris. I still had the freedom to travel when I wanted and the freedom to experience new things, but with two people I loved.

Our new life wasn't perfect. Amy and Freddie must have feared that I'd do it again, and I did still have to fight the impulse to let my fear (or my ego) take over. But we got through every challenge and our relationship flourished. We spent more time together and even started planning for another addition to the family. Things were getting more serious and I was growing up.

My role as a stepdad taught me new lessons every day. My love for Freddie grew with every goodnight kiss I gave him. I never would have pictured myself living this life. I might have seen myself as a successful entrepreneur sitting on a yacht or driving fancy cars! But not this. And yet, this life felt so much more meaningful.

I felt a tug at my heartstrings every time Freddie said, 'I have two dads.' Fortunately, the initial awkwardness went away and I got on well with Freddie's dad. I had to hand it to him and Amy – they'd had some challenges along the way but still managed to co-parent well, and they always put Freddie's needs first.

I always treated Freddie as my own. I didn't call him my stepson – he was my son. Even though I missed the first 20 months of his life, I felt like I'd been there from the beginning, and he did too.

Freddie gave my life more meaning and he gave me so much more hope for the future. Just the fact that he saw me as his dad motivated me to consistently better myself. Not just for me, but for him. I couldn't let things slip. I couldn't go back to how I was. And I couldn't ever do what Dad had done.

CHAPTER 13

WHEN EVERYTHING
IS NOT ENOUGH

I felt ready. I wanted to have a baby with Amy. I wanted to give Freddie the brother or sister he said he wanted. After talking it through, we started trying, and in the back of my mind I expected it to take a few months for anything to really happen.

There was still some fear attached to it: the fear of being a dad, the fear of being able to go through the pregnancy, and of dealing with a newborn – something I had never done before. And underneath all of that was the pain that my dad would not be there to see his grandchild.

After the first few weeks of trying, Amy took the test ... when she saw the result a smile spread across her face. She was pregnant. She looked at me and my expression didn't match hers. Fuck. This was something I had wanted to happen. It was something I'd expected, but the result put me into shock. I didn't think it would be that quick. I couldn't quite take it in.

My reaction obviously scared Amy. One minute we had been planning it excitedly and I had been telling her that I was ready for it. And then, as soon as we got the good news, there wasn't any joy, just panic. I tried to explain it to her.

I told her I was just shocked at how quickly it happened and she told me she understood.

That night we celebrated. I was really excited to tell Mum and I thought it would hopefully bring some joy to her life. Mum was over the moon. She really wanted to become a nan before she turned 50!

As the news started to sink in, I found I couldn't wipe the smile off my face. My life was about to change for ever, our family was about to change, we were going to have a baby. Even though it was only a few weeks into the pregnancy, we started planning ahead. We booked an early six-week scan at a private clinic to make sure everything was okay, but also because we wanted to share the good news with more people.

On the day of the scan, we went in and were so excited to see our little baby's heartbeat. The scan didn't show one.

They told us it looked like an ectopic pregnancy, and if it was, the pregnancy wouldn't be successful. But the lady doing the scan said it was still so early and it was quite hard to tell for sure. We both left upset, but Amy more so than me. I still held onto some hope that it would be okay, but she found it hard to stay hopeful. A few weeks later she miscarried.

It took some time to heal. Seeing Amy have to go through that – physically as well as mentally – was horrible. We had to start to consider that we might not be able to have a baby of our own. Neither of us had expected that. Amy had fallen pregnant quickly with Freddie, so why was this happening? We had just assumed everything would go swimmingly, but we were being naïve.

It took us a while to recover. But in time we decided to try again. But this time, we struggled to fall pregnant. And the next time. And the next ...

As every month passed and with every negative pregnancy test, our dreams of having a baby faded away. We decided to get help. We travelled to a private clinic to see what they could do to help. The lady was compassionate and she advised us to try a few things to help with conception. Amy made a few changes, I was advised to stop wearing such tight-fitting jeans, and gradually, things started to change.

After another year of trying, Amy fell pregnant again. With the news of her being pregnant bringing joy to us all, we started to talk about moving into a bigger house. We could've made do in the flat we were in, but I wanted to provide something bigger for them. I wanted to give my family the life they deserved. We spent a few nights looking online and found one we both liked, but it was taken off the market quickly. It would have been too good to be true anyway, so we both let it go. A week later I browsed again and saw that it was back on the market. We went to see it that afternoon, with Freddie and a baby in Amy's tummy, and put down a deposit the morning after.

We moved into the new house and our future looked exciting. The bond between the three of us was stronger than ever, Amy was pregnant, and we'd just moved into a dream home. But then it happened again. We went to our six-week scan to make sure everything was okay. But it wasn't. Again, we lost the baby.

Seeing Amy having to endure another miscarriage was hard and I often wished I could take on the pain myself. This lack of control hurt me. I couldn't do anything to help her get through it and that ate away at me. At the same time, I was struggling to deal with the loss myself ... silently. Amy was going through far worse than me and I felt I couldn't get upset in front of her. I needed to be the rock and try to give her the optimism she needed to keep trying. There were times when Amy didn't want to continue trying and I understood that. But I desperately wanted a baby. The "dream" was turning into a nightmare. With more time to recover, we tried again.

This time, conceiving didn't take as long. But yet again we lost the baby.

With every miscarriage, I saw Amy endure more pain. We both knew that the only way we could stop this pain would be to stop trying for a baby. She couldn't go through this again.

We went back to see the lady who had helped us before. She advised giving it another go with some additional medication to help get us past that six-week stage. After trying again, Amy fell pregnant.

The news of her being pregnant always excited us, but we always had that dreadful worry that we might be heading for another miscarriage. By this stage, conceiving wasn't the hard part, getting past six weeks of pregnancy was.

With ongoing support from the clinic, and with Amy now on steroids and daily injections, the six-week scan showed a heartbeat. So did the seven-week scan. So did the eight-week scan. And the ninth ...

This time, it looked as if everything was going to be okay with the pregnancy and we paid for an early gender scan to find out that Freddie was going to have a little brother.

Another boy.

We were both elated with the news.

With the news now publicly announced that we were having a baby, everything in life seemed to be looking up. That "dream" life I always expected of myself was playing out. My online fashion retail business was doing well. I was running an online men's fashion magazine, I was consulting for a successful seven-figure online business, and I was running a short course lecture series at the London College of Fashion. I was making more money than ever before. I was exercising and eating well, and I had more friends than I'd ever had before. Life was good. I'd sit on the sofa sometimes and just look out to the garden, thinking, I've done it. The house wasn't a mansion by any means and we were only renting, but I felt like I was giving Amy, Freddie, and our future children the life they'd want.

From the outside, things looked to be going well and I was thinking about proposing to Amy – but there was still something missing. I felt like I wasn't "enough". Even with the success of the business, I wanted more. I was making money, but I wanted more. I felt like I wasn't good enough as a dad, partner, son, brother, grandson, or friend. In reality I had most of what I had always wanted, but I didn't feel like I had enough.

Why was I still having days when I felt so low, anxious, isolated, and lonely? There were times when I'd shut off from Amy and Freddie altogether, and times where I'd get angry, frustrated, or irritated very quickly. I'd opened up to Ann; I thought I'd dealt with Dad and everything I'd been feeling but now I had become obsessed with feeling better, always chasing some new hack to make me into a better person. I was running again, running away from the issue, and distracting myself with achievements. But I couldn't stop the constant chase for more.

And with all of that going on, the single hardest thought I battled was the fear I might still end up like my dad. I had too much to live for now, too many people relying on me.

I found myself spiralling down into depression again and deeper into debt. I was struggling to pay for the extravagant lifestyle that I thought made us all happy. We'd moved from a two-bed flat to a five-bed house, with a lifestyle to match. But I couldn't let Amy and Freddie down – I knew I had to continue doing everything I could to keep our lifestyle going, to make sure we could eat out, and go on holidays ... and there was an engagement ring to buy, and a baby to save for ...

I didn't want to tell Amy though, I couldn't. It would have felt like letting her down.

There was a specific moment when I knew I needed to get help once again. An argument with Amy. I can't even remember what the argument was about, but I found myself shouting, punching a door, and then running down the stairs in just my boxer shorts, and pacing around the utility room, shaking. I couldn't catch my breath, I couldn't shut my thoughts off, I felt like I was going to do something stupid. Moments like this always brought me back to the thought that had haunted me ever since Dad died ... Could I do it too? Was I capable of doing what my dad had done?

I slowed my breathing down and kept telling myself that it was going to be okay, over and over again. I laid out on the sofa, calming down, bit by bit, before I took myself up to bed. I still couldn't understand why I was feeling all that uncertainty, all that pain. I knew I had so much to live for; I couldn't understand why I wasn't feeling on top of the world.

I went to see Ann and told her how I was feeling. We talked it through and it started to become clear that I needed to start focusing on myself again. I'd let the good habits slip that had helped me get out of the dark hole the last time. (Even now, a week of neglecting the things that make me feel good about myself can have a massive impact on my feelings.)

Ann reminded me to accept who I was and what I had, or else I'd always be chasing more. She quoted a line that has stuck with me ever since:

'Success is getting what you want. Happiness is wanting what you get.'

Within a few days of taking her advice and focusing on myself, I started to feel better. I also kept repeating that quote to myself over and over. I had always thought that getting what I wanted would make me happy. I'd thought it would simply clear away the fear that I could break down and take my own life like Dad had, but it didn't. My happiness needed to come first, not the achievements that I was chasing. And that happiness needed to come from within, not from the things I was achieving or buying.

I knew that my fear of ending up like my dad was a fear I had to accept, as well as being something that I had to move beyond. I couldn't bear to inflict the same pain I had gone through on my family, and with the added responsibilities coming my way, the fear started to increase. Somehow, I had to get through it. I had to overcome it.

I had to realise something important: everything I have is already enough.

CHAPTER 14

BEING DAD

The sun was shining and there were more than 20 kids at our house celebrating Freddie's birthday. There was a bouncy castle in the garden, pokeballs scattered around the house, Freddie was running around pretending to be Ash Ketchum, and I was just starting to question why I'd put myself through it all over again! But the smile on Freddie's face made it all worthwhile.

Amy cut the two-tier Pokemon cake (featuring Pikachu and Bulbasaur, of course), bringing another party to an end for another year. It was all her hard work. She planned and pulled off every party brilliantly. I helped out where I needed to, and always ended up joining in like a big kid by the end of it.

But this party was just a bit different. Amy was heavily pregnant and the due date was just three days away. We'd been wondering if the little man would come on Freddie's birthday. We'd got a home birth scheduled, and we'd been joking about clearing kids and parents out of the house if Amy suddenly went into labour. I'd been brushing it off, saying I could set up the birthing pool upstairs and she could give birth there without anyone knowing. 'It's easy, right? This childbirth thing?' I joked. In return, I got the look. You know, "the look".

Amy's mum had already told me, 'Today will be the day,' but I shrugged it off. We'd been saying, 'Today is the day,' for a week now.

With every child and parent out of the house, we tidied up and settled down. Luckily, the sugar had left Freddie's system and he went to bed at a good time. We lay upstairs in our bedroom, watching Netflix. We hadn't eaten much through the day, so I went downstairs to rustle up my finest meal of southern fried chicken cooked from frozen! Just before the 20-minute timer went off, and just before I was about to plate up our tasty chicken with a side of ketchup, it happened.

'PAUL!' came the cry from upstairs. I went running up there to find her out of bed and in the bathroom. 'My waters have broken! My waters didn't break with Freddie. I DIDN'T EXPECT MY WATERS TO BREAK!' I saw the panic on her face.

'Don't panic,' I told her uncertainly, putting some towels down on the floor. 'Let me ring your mum.'

I was fine. Definitely not panicking! I got Amy's mum on the phone and shouted, 'AMY'S WATERS HAVE BROKEN AND IT'S HAPPENING!' No, not panicking. Just absolutely shitting myself. Amy's mum told me to calm down.

We were all set up for a home birth, so it was my job to get the bathing pool set up while Amy called the midwife. I laid out the birthing pool and all of the equipment in the living room, and began pumping it up. We still hadn't really tested it out, so I battled with all kinds of worrying thoughts as I quickly scanned through the instruction manual.

It struck me as funny. Just a few hours earlier, kids had been running around in this living room throwing pokeballs ... now my son was about to be born here.

I could hear Amy walking down the stairs talking to the midwife. Her panic had been replaced by sadness; they didn't have any midwives available to come out for the home birth.

With Amy's contractions coming so close together, we were told to go straight to hospital. Amy had her mind set on a home birth. She'd been using the hypnobirthing techniques we'd learnt and visualised how she thought it would happen. But that wasn't going to happen.

As soon as Amy got off the phone, she broke into tears. This really wasn't a good start. Her mum arrived – she was going to be Amy's birth partner – and my mum came over to babysit Freddie. I knew we weren't going to have the sort of experience we'd been expecting, but I grabbed the hypnobirthing CD on the way out.

Amy was really uncomfortable, so I drove as carefully but as fast as I could. As this was her second birth, we both feared it could happen before we even got to the hospital. The hypnobirthing music helped. Even though Amy was in a lot of pain, she was managing to breathe deeply and stay calm. Hypnobirthing was paying off already.

We made it to the hospital and I bundled in with all the bags, including the cool bag ready for the placenta after the birth. I knew it was supposed to be a good thing to do, but I was just weirded out at the word placenta. Amy was all wrapped up, trying to protect herself, just in case her waters broke again. But I looked as if I was ready for a trip to the beach, wearing a T-shirt, short shorts, and flip-flops – and carrying a cool bag.

We were lucky to get a private room with a birthing pool, and the midwife on shift was really nice. She made Amy feel welcome and she was completely open about the hypnobirthing process. As it was one of the hottest days of the year, the room we were in was extremely stuffy. Amy lay down on the floor on a medium-sized cushion; it didn't look comfortable or ideal. My visions of Amy giving birth in our lovely house, with snacks and cool drinks at the ready, had been replaced by the reality of Amy lying on a hospital floor.

I held her hand and tried to comfort her as much as I could, while her mum rubbed her back, and we listened to a playlist of relaxing music we'd created. The panic of an imminent birth died down. The midwife assessed her and told her it could be a while. That relaxed Amy a little bit, and even though she was obviously uncomfortable, she seemed to be doing well.

As time went on, her contractions got more painful and the nausea came on. She felt sick and dehydrated. Throughout it all, even as she was being violently sick while experiencing more and more painful contractions, she did all she could to stay calm.

The dehydration was a problem, but Amy just couldn't keep any liquid down. The midwife took alternative action. 'You're going to have to eat some jam,' she said. 'Raspberry or strawberry?' It didn't work – and Amy hasn't touched jam since that day. I just didn't know what to expect. Through eight hours of labour – Amy wants me to point out that the labour with Freddie lasted 24 hours – the way in which Amy dealt with it just blew me away. She stayed calm, she used the techniques we learnt in hypnobirthing, and she went as long as possible without the use of gas and air. There was one time though when I let go of her hand for a second and she grabbed her mum's hair, pulled it, and didn't let go for a good few seconds. I'll never forget her mum's face – she was shocked but she knew she couldn't say anything to Amy. I just wanted to laugh but I kept it together.

By the time they moved Amy to the birthing pool, all sorts of thoughts were racing through my mind. *Will Amy be okay? Will the baby be okay? What is he going to look like? What if the scan was wrong and it's a girl?*

For what seemed like hours to me and probably felt like days to Amy, it happened. He was here. The midwife pulled him up out of the water and laid him on Amy's chest. My eyes started welling up and I struggled to breathe in.

Shit!

He was here. Even though he was covered in white gunk, had a squashed face, and was crying on Amy's chest in the birthing pool ... he was beautiful. I couldn't believe that, after all of that time, after the pain of the miscarriages, and truly doubting that this would ever happen, he was with us at last.

The midwife said he'd already been following in his daddy's footsteps, by wrapping his cord around his neck on the way out!

I think relief was the word to describe that moment. Relief that it was over and relief that he and Amy were both okay. After a minute or two they took him away to assess him, and I went and stood over him. I stared into his eyes. I still can't describe the feelings that ran through me. Life had again changed for ever.

'Pick him up and give him a cuddle, Daddy,' the midwife told me. I just stared at him and said, 'I have no idea how ...' I had hoped that by being a stepdad, this newborn thing would be easy. Not knowing how to even pick him up wasn't a good start. Amy's mum helped me, and as I cradled him in my arms, I promised to myself to never let him down (or drop him). I welled up again and saw Amy looking over at me, smiling.

Amy needed more assessments after giving birth. She'd done all the hard work and our baby had been whisked away for me to play with. But we were soon together again, just holding him and staring at him with so much love.

Teddie Harry McGregor-Galliford was born on 18th July 2016 at 2.30am.

Our family became four. My life became more.

CHAPTER 15

FINDING MEANING

I thought being a new dad was going to be a walk in the park. But as the weeks went on I really started to see how different fathering a newborn was to being a stepdad to a young child. I was already regretting having shown no interest in the pre-natal classes. But Amy taught me everything I needed to know: from changing a nappy to being able to hold him comfortably while standing up (before that, I'd only ever held babies sitting down).

It wasn't always easy. Because Amy needed to show me everything, it caused a bit of conflict between us. My ego took a battering every time she helped me with him, and I often got annoyed with her (and myself) when I struggled to do what needed to be done. I wanted to be a hands-on dad but found I was making a lot of mistakes, whether it was washing the bottles with the wrong sponge or feeding him his bottle at the wrong angle. Amy was already very used to doing those things for Freddie and so inevitably it was easier for her to try to do it all, but I wanted to get as hands-on as possible.

But learning from those mistakes and with us working a balance, it wasn't long before I felt completely comfortable with him. I felt like I could look after him, cater to his every need, and provide for him. The feeling of being able to feed your child, stop your child from crying, make your child laugh, and provide a loving environment for him is hard to beat.

The next few months were some of the most joyful but also some of the most challenging. I was reminded that the biggest rewards in life are often connected to big challenges along the way. I would do everything I could for Teddie. I just wanted to see him happy, but to get that reward meant overcoming challenges. It meant changing shitty nappies, having restless nights, dealing with tears, and getting baby sick on my fresh new camel overcoat.

For the first few months, our routine was fairly non-existent. Work became less of a priority and I struggled to feel inspired to do anything creative. A lot of what I was doing before Teddie was born went on hold, and I found it hard at times. I wasn't exercising much, I was eating badly, I didn't have much time for myself to read or meditate, and where I'd enjoyed my work before, I was now finding it a bit of a chore.

I wish Dad was here to see him.

I couldn't help thinking that. When my grandad met him for the first time, he immediately said he looked like my dad.

It was a constant battle – balancing the joyful times to then feeling hurt and saddened that my dad wasn't around.

I felt that sadness really strongly one night. It was around 2.00am and as I was giving him his bottle in his cot, I stared at him and the sadness washed over me in waves. 'How could my dad do this to me?' I asked. 'How could he do it to my brother?' Being a dad had brought so many joyful emotions but had also got me questioning my dad once again. I felt some anger towards him, but most of all, I was sad that he could leave his children. And now his grandchild.

I found myself again trying to relive that moment he stepped in front of a lorry. I wondered if I could have done that. There was a part of me that thought I could, but there was a stronger urge that told me to do all I could to never let that happen.

I finished feeding him and got back into bed. I turned my back to Amy – I didn't want her to see me or hear me – and then the tears started to come. There was a slight gap in the curtain and I looked up to the sky. The stars were shining bright but I still felt that huge sense of remorse. There were times when Teddie was born where I felt able to be honest about my dad not being there, when I spoke about him openly and wanted Teddie to know his grandad would've loved him. But in that moment, I hated him for leaving us.

The next morning, I woke to Amy feeding Teddie his morning bottle and Freddie lying in bed with us. I looked through the gap in the curtain again. The sky was bright with the possibilities of a new day and this time I smiled. I sat on those thoughts over the next few days and spoke to my mum about them. I told Amy that I was struggling to deal with Dad not being around too, but I didn't want to tell her everything, I didn't want to scare her. Looking back, I wish I had been braver. I know that she would have understood and helped me deal with those feelings. But the old version of me crept back in, telling me I would be weak if I told her, telling me she might even leave me ...

As the weeks and months went on, I started to find myself being able to manage those emotions more. I was embracing them and understanding that it was normal for me to feel them. What new dad wouldn't want their dad to be with them, playing an active, physical role in their son's life?

We were starting to settle as a family of four. I was finding a nice balance between family time and "me" time, my drive for work had started to come back, and I was doing a lot of the things that made me feel good. As the nights got longer and as Teddie got bigger, it gave me more time to think.

My life has more meaning now.

I'd been struggling to motivate myself before Teddie was born. I'd lost a sense of purpose in the work I'd been doing. I'd read somewhere that motivation comes from meaning. When you understand the meaning behind what you do, it drives you. It's the reminder you need when you're about to give up or just not do it at all. I'd experienced that feeling before, after losing Dad. I'd had that drive and motivation to set up my online business. It felt then as if everything I did was driven by my need to make him proud.

And when my relationship with Amy had started getting more serious and I had started playing a more active role in Freddie's life, I found I had more motivation then too. It wasn't just about me making money to fund my nights out and my lifestyle aspirations, I had the motivation to work hard to give Amy and Freddie the best possible life.

As time went on, I found that the motivation and drive inevitably reduces, whatever you're doing. I think that's true for all of us. But the meaning behind why I was doing it helped me stay strong. Any time I lack motivation now, I close my eyes and think of my family. It is about more than just me. Whether it's trying to motivate myself to wake up at 5.00am to write or pushing through the final minute of an intense run, every time I feel like saying no or giving up, I remind myself of why I'm doing it.

As the months went by, I started to feel better than I'd ever felt. Our family felt complete, I was settling in as a dad, and my relationship with Freddie grew stronger too. I had been a little bit worried about how having Teddie would affect my relationship with Freddie, but if anything, it made it stronger. He was now the big brother and in the early days of our new family life, when Teddie really needed his mum, I found myself spending more time with Freddie. Freddie has a great relationship with his biological dad – I really respect the active role he plays in Freddie's life and I never intend to break that. But I have two boys now. Not one and a half, or one biological son and a stepson. I'm a father of two.

I'd heard a lot about the book *Man's Search for Meaning* and bought it before Teddie was born. But I didn't get around to reading it until Teddie was about five months old. When I did, everything I was feeling – my new drive and motivation, my feeling like life was about more than just me – all clicked.

Man's Search for Meaning is a 1946 book by Viktor Frankl, which documents his experiences as an Auschwitz concentration camp inmate during World War Two. He describes the coping techniques he used to get through it, which involved identifying a purpose in life, something for him to feel positively about, and then impressively imagining that outcome.

This was one of the key points that stood out for me: *Man's main concern is not to gain pleasure or to avoid pain but rather to see a meaning in his life.*

As soon as I read this, I thought about Dad. Was it a lack of meaning and purpose in his life that was the reason he had killed himself? Why wasn't his family a strong enough reason for him to live? Or maybe he just lost that meaning.

The book really struck a chord with how I was feeling. As more reasons to live stacked up, from making my dad proud, to giving Amy, Freddie and Teddie the best life I could, I found myself feeling more driven and more fulfilled than ever before.

I'd used to think it was a bit of a cliché when someone told me they were driven by something else, something other than their own gain, but all of a sudden, I found myself doing exactly that. There were days where I'd lack motivation and days where I'd find it hard to get out of bed in the morning, but knowing why I was alive and being able to attach so much more meaning to the things I did made everything easier.

Digging back into my lowest moments – to the depression and to the suicidal thoughts I'd experienced – they were all at times when I had lacked meaning in my life. Times when I hadn't had a purpose to stay alive or be happy. Times when all I could think about was the pain of losing Dad, the need to want to see him again, and my anger towards him.

My depression had come from a lack of meaning in life. My meaning at that time was to make Dad proud, but that was something I couldn't fulfil because he was no longer alive. Before that, my meaning had been to make money so that I could gain status. But that hadn't been enough to keep me happy either.

Without meaning in your life, it's difficult to see any kind of a future.

I started to see other people's lives in those ways too. I heard about a friend of mine taking his own life. We had been close at school. We had both been into music and spent evenings messing around on the turntables. We'd drifted apart when we left school but I still saw him on occasion, just not as much. I hadn't seen him for a while when I heard the news ...

He had hanged himself in his bedroom.

He had been so young. He'd had so much opportunity in front of him, but from the inside he must have been telling himself a different story.

I remembered someone from school who had lost his dad to suicide as well. Again, from the outside you'd have thought his dad had every reason to stay alive. Although I'd thought it was bad at the time, I'd quickly got on with my life. It was one of those stories that you hear, you feel empathy, and then you quickly move on. It's a story you never think will happen to you. But after Dad died, it prompted me to get in touch with that guy through Facebook. We hadn't spoken much at school, but all of a sudden we had something in common and I needed his help. I wanted to know how he had handled it.

I then became more aware of other people I knew who were depressed. After my dad died, lots of them started freely opening up to me. Some of them shared their own stories of people they had lost through suicide.

I started to become more aware of suicide in the news and on social media too. I remember a time when the commuters from London to my home town were complaining they couldn't get home because some "idiot" had jumped in front of the train. This selfish "idiot" caused them to be late for the gym and miss the football or the pub. The insensitive jokes followed.

It reminded me that we all have suicide potential. We all have some proclivity for self-murder, which can come from our past experiences and the way we're conditioned. It's a scary thought. A thought we're mostly unconscious to. And studies show that if you've been exposed to suicide there's a higher risk of taking your own life too.

This was and still is one of my biggest fears – I fear I'll end up like my dad. You already know I've been very close.

When I've spoken to men who have thought about suicide, I'm always intrigued by what held them back – why they didn't go through with it and why my dad did.

Whether it was a reminder of their family or their children, or someone who managed to tell them the thing they needed to hear at the time, or even sensing something bigger than them (whether that was God or something else external to them), it showed me how important meaning was to our lives.

It's still upsetting to know that Dad didn't have any meaning to stay alive, and that the impulse to end his pain and depression outweighed his reasons to live. I just wish I had known this back then. I wish I could have showed him he had a purpose in life. I wish I could have shown him how loved he was, how supported he was, how much so many people needed him to be alive.

I honestly think my dad could still be alive. He could still be alive if he could have just had that glimmer of hope. To be reminded of how much meaning he had in his life and just how much he meant to us.

I want to be the best son to my mum. I want to be the best brother to Steve. I want to be the best partner to Amy. I want to be the best dad to Freddie and Teddie. And that's why I know I need to work on bettering myself every day.

Suicide is all around us. Depression is rising but it's still something we refrain from talking about. Why whisper the word "suicide" but still find it funny to joke about it freely? Why is something that affects so many of us still stigmatised? Why can't we talk about it openly? Those were the questions I still needed answers for.

Those who have a why to live, can bear with almost any how.

– Viktor Frankl (quoting Friedrich Nietzsche
in *Man's Search for Meaning*)

CHAPTER 16

FROM KRAKOW
TO TUSCANY

'So when are you getting married then, Paul?' people would ask. We'd been living as a family of three and then a family of four – we had the relationship, the family home, the 5-door car ... but we weren't Mr and Mrs.

Amy had always wanted to get married – especially to someone like me of course! And I'd thought about popping the question for a while but I found myself having huge doubts about it.

There was never a question over whether I wanted to marry Amy or not, but I struggled to see myself getting married without my dad being there. I traced back to a few days after Dad died. I was in my bedroom looking out of the window, in tears. Thoughts were racing through my head about everything he would miss: seeing me become a dad, seeing his sons growing up, being there to support Mum ... and being there at my wedding.

I just didn't know if I could face getting married without Dad being there. When Amy started to question why I didn't want to get married, I was open with her about it. She understood how

I felt, we talked it through, and I knew that it was what I wanted more than anything else in the world, and I was ready to pop the question.

Luckily, Amy didn't like public attention. The thought of me proposing to her in a restaurant or in a crowded area made her anxious. She wanted something more thoughtful at home and something that involved Freddie. I decided to put my very average video editing talents to use and created a video for her a week before I proposed. The video involved me and Freddie dancing to Bruno Mars' 'Marry You'. (Yes, I know. Reading that just made you cringe – especially if you've seen me dance – but adding a six-year-old into the dance routine turned it from "cringey" to "cute".)

The dance routine transitioned into a video of me upstairs, getting dressed into a suit. You then saw me walk downstairs, stand by the living room door, reach into my suit pocket, and then the video faded out. Everything went white and the music transitioned into one of our favourite Ed Sheeran songs, 'Tenerife Sea'. There were photos of us animated on the video and then text appeared on the screen telling her to close her eyes.

When she got home from work one day, Freddie and I sat her down. We played the video and I went upstairs to get ready. Freddie waited to hear the song transition, walked in, held her hand, and led her into the middle of the room. She stood there with her eyes closed as I entered the room, got down on one knee, and told her to open her eyes. Freddie was kneeling too, on one knee, mirroring everything I was doing. As I waited for her response, I felt slightly anxious that she wouldn't like the proposal, but inside I knew she'd say yes!

With the wedding plans in full swing, Amy took control. If either of us was going to plan the perfect wedding, it would be her. I decided to take the role of the nodding dog, saying, 'Yes, sounds good,' when she'd show me something or, 'Ooh, no, sounds expensive,' when she'd show me something extravagant.

With both our families being quite small, we wanted to keep things intimate. I knew that if we invited all of our friends and partners it would take away that family element. So we decided on a wedding at an amazing villa called Villa San Crispolto, just outside Tuscany in Italy.

But a few weeks before we flew to Italy, I found myself handcuffed, blindfolded, and kidnapped from my bed at 5.00am. Don't worry, I was fine. I was simply being whisked away on my stag do. Two nights in Krakow, Poland, all organised by Steve (who was also my best man), with my close friends and with Amy's full cooperation.

We drove five minutes and got out the car. I still couldn't see a thing. It's a funny feeling hearing everyone talk, knowing people are looking at you, but not being able to see what's going on. As we got on a minibus, they removed the handcuffs and blindfold. When I opened my eyes I saw every one of them staring back at me wearing a cardboard mask of my face.

I didn't tell them this at the time but it made them all 10 times more attractive for the few seconds they wore them!

We were staying in the most budget-conscious hotel they could find. I had to wear a colourful comedy tracksuit and a curly black wig, and we headed out to hunt down the cheapest pub. We found ourselves in a "certain" bar offering unlimited beer for the equivalent of £10.00. It wasn't quite the dream we were sold – the staff had no hesitation in showing us that we weren't really wanted in there. They told us we had to keep our glasses if we wanted to keep topping them up.

A bit self-consciously, we all huddled into a booth and drank. After an hour or so one of my friends, through pure frustration, decided to punch a wall in the bar. He quickly realised that the wall was merely made from a thin sheet of plasterboard, as his fist sank through the whole wall. As soon as we saw him do it, we knew we needed to get out of there before they noticed. But by the time we made our way down to the exit, they had locked the doors. We were trapped.

This was the moment when I realised just how drunk I was as I stood on the steps pretending to phone the British Embassy and telling the club security men that our Embassy was coming to save us. For some reason, it didn't work. And neither did the shouting at them to let us out.

With tension escalating, one of my mates got sprayed in the eyes. Then they started spraying anyone else who looked like they were getting out of hand. They sprayed me too. That's when I realised it wasn't foam. It was pepper spray.

My eyes started to burn. It felt like someone had rubbed the hottest chilli in my eyes and I couldn't open them. Some of the guys managed to settle up the money we owed for the wall and they opened the doors, letting us spill out onto the streets while screaming in pain.

Believe it or not, I'd never been pepper sprayed before. It was an experience I wouldn't wish on my worst enemy. I splashed my face with water to try to wash it out, but it just dripped down my body, taking some of the foam with it. I mean, literally, all the way down. My eyes were on fire and now, you guessed it, so were my balls.

I ripped my top off, trying to use it as a towel to rub my eyes. What must I have looked like? Careering blindly down a busy street in Krakow, topless, and still wearing my colourful tracksuit trousers. The guys who hadn't been sprayed escorted us back to the hotel and we jumped in showers, trying to wash the foam away. In time, my eyes started to open. My body was still tingling but the burning sensation had gone. It definitely sobered us up and definitely ruined the mood. Lesson learnt.

Sobered up and fresh-eyed, I spent some of the next day on a shooting range, dressed in a corset and tutu. More drinks and more laughs followed, and by the time we made it home, we had plenty of stories to tell. (But the pepper spray story couldn't be beaten!)

A couple of weeks later, we flew out for the wedding itself. The villa was breathtaking: the view, the rooms, the grounds, the pool, and the plentiful alcohol meant we were in for a good week. The day before the showcase wedding, Amy and I went to Cortona, a town about 30 minutes away, with Marco, the owner of the villa, and two friends as witnesses to officially register our wedding. It was a surreal moment, with the lady in the town hall reading the legal stuff in her thick Italian accent. And with that, we were married. We laughed and kissed, and everyone clapped. We knew that the wedding the next day would make it feel official but on paper we were already husband and wife.

I woke up on the wedding day alone. Amy had slept in the wedding suite with her best friend and maid of honour. The nerves were contained and I was simply just looking forward to the day ahead.

It was strange not being able to see Amy, but I'd shout up at her whenever I walked past the wedding suite where she was getting her hair and make-up done, and she'd shout back. It was almost like she was a princess trapped in a castle and I was the handsome, strong prince who had come to rescue her. Actually, scratch that masculine power story! She was definitely the one who saved me.

I was still keeping the emotions in check. But by the time I saw the little boys – Freddie, Teddie, and our best friend's son, Jack – in their white grandad collar shirts, navy shorts, braces, and brown loafers (to match the men's) I started to feel just a bit emotional. How was I going to feel when I saw Amy?

We made our way up to the top of the villa where the wedding ceremony was going to take place. We had to walk past the pool to get there and wearing a three piece suit in the Italian summer made it tempting to jump in to cool off.

The guests took their seats, with Mum and the other guests sitting behind me. I stood facing the front with Steve, and then the kids started to walk down the aisle. First came Abbi, Amy's maid of honour, with her two children, Jack and Amelia, and I could feel the tears forming. Then came Freddie carrying Teddie, and my eyes started to well up. They looked so cute and I was so proud of them both. I gave Teddie a cuddle and told him I loved him before passing him to Amy's mum, and then I cuddled Freddie and told him I loved him too. I wiped the tears from my eyes and tried to keep it together. I hadn't even seen Amy yet. Then the music started – we'd chosen 'Tenerife Sea' by Ed Sheeran, the song from my proposal video. We'd heard it at one of our first concerts together and hearing it again, as Amy walked towards me, just made me well up again as I thought through the happy times we had spent together.

Amy looked so beautiful. Smiling back at me, I could see she was slightly nervous too, but seeing her made me feel much more at ease. Her dad walked with her towards me. This was it. The wedding we'd both been waiting for.

Amy looked happy as I read out the vow I had written for her. She laughed at some of the funnier points and softly said, 'That's sweet,' so nobody could hear her apart from me.

It was Amy's turn next and I didn't know what to expect. We'd been joking beforehand about whose vow would be better, and we'd both agreed to make them light-hearted. Amy's two sides of A4 paper, compared with my one side of A5, already put her in the lead. I listened closely to every word, taking it all in as she said it. Her vows reinforced every feeling I had towards her. It was funny, but more importantly, supportive of everything I am.

I knew I was marrying someone who brought out the best in me. And now I felt like I knew I brought out the best in her too. I thought the years of me writing might mean my vows would swing the competition, but hands down, there was no competition.

The wedding day was better than expected. It was everything we ever imagined and more. I remember waking up in the morning and wanting to do it all over again. It was time to start our lives as husband and wife.

CHAPTER 17

DAYS THAT CHANGE LIVES

We still had two more days to spend at the villa, so we used that time to relax, explore, and overindulge in the amazing Italian food and drink. We flew back on the Saturday, with everyone seeming quite deflated to be back in England.

Wearing a ring still felt very new. I kept looking at it and twisting it around my finger. I'd never really worn jewellery and obviously I'd never been married, so this ring signified something really meaningful. That evening we were all tired, so we snuggled up on the sofa as a family of four and ordered a takeaway.

We'd just had the most amazing week in a breathtaking Italian villa so it took a few days to get back into our normal routine. I knew exercise would be a way to get me out of the holiday blues, so a few days after getting back I went for an early workout. I then headed down to the coffee shop to catch up with some work. I stayed there for an hour or two and as I was leaving I saw I had a missed call and voicemail from my mum. Straightaway that seemed strange. Mum almost always texted me and she never left voicemails. I thought something was wrong.

I called her back as I was driving home and I could hear the panic in her voice. Scared of the answer, I asked her what was wrong. 'Steve's been in an accident at work,' she said. 'His boss called – he told me not to worry, but he's had a head injury.' She said that Steve was conscious and talking, but he was being airlifted to Royal London Hospital as a precaution.

Her boss had assured Mum that Steve was going to be okay, but we hurried to the hospital. We assumed he'd be kept in overnight with concussion, so Mum had packed him an overnight bag. We asked at reception where we'd find him and they told us he'd been taken to resus. My heart rate quickened. Wasn't that where they resuscitated people? Mum reassured me though. She told me it was where people went if they'd been brought in by air ambulance. She'd watched a lot of *Casualty* on TV.

Steve's boss and one his colleagues came to meet us at the hospital while we waited to see Steve. I couldn't help worrying that he hadn't been telling Mum the whole story on the phone, and as soon as I went to meet him on my own, I blurted out, 'Be honest with me, is it worse than you made out to Mum?'

Steve's boss replied, 'It's not looking good. I'm sorry.'

My heart sank. 'But you said he was conscious ...' He went on to explain that some steel from a hoist had fallen onto the top of Steve's head, but he assured me the paramedics had confirmed his skull was intact, and he had been able to respond and answer questions. That reassured me a bit. At least he had been conscious the whole time. I led them into the hospital to where Mum was waiting. After about 20 minutes, someone asked for the relatives of Steven McGregor, and led me and Mum into a private room.

As we went in to see the surgeon and two of the nurses, I tried to breathe deeply and think positively. The surgeon said, 'I've been operating on Steven for the past few hours. He has very serious damage to the brain.' He didn't need to say any more. This was bad. They looked sad; they looked sorry for us.

'Steve has fractured his skull badly, in fact it's probably the worst skull fracture I've seen.' Sensitivity obviously wasn't the surgeon's strong point. 'I've managed to remove the pieces of skull that had shattered and reduce some of the bleeding, but it really isn't looking good ...'

I broke down, Mum broke down ... why was this happening to us again?

'But he's not going to die?' Mum asked, wiping the tears from her eyes. The reply was stark. 'There's a possibility that he could.'

I pulled Mum close. The tears were running down my face but I tried to hold back the panic. I tried to control my breathing and stared at the wall directly in front of me. I needed to be strong for Mum. She needed that from me now.

They didn't say anything else for a good 30 seconds. They just looked on sadly as we held onto each other and tried to take it all in. Just six days ago, Steve had handed me the ring as the best man at my wedding – but now ... I couldn't make sense of it. What had we done to deserve this?

They told us what had happened in more detail. The paramedics had sedated Steve before getting him into the air ambulance because he'd been getting agitated and confused, a sign that the swelling on his brain was getting more dangerous. Before that, they had given him a consciousness score of 14 out of 15. That felt like a positive, but didn't mean much in the grand scheme of things. Because he'd been airlifted to the hospital, they'd been able to operate on him within a couple of hours of the accident. That was pretty unheard of and we were grateful that he'd been looked after so quickly.

Steve's skull had shattered in the accident, spreading small pieces around his brain. The surgeon had had to remove each piece. The brain had bled and started to swell, and so they'd had to remove some more of the skull to try and relieve the pressure. They'd put him into an induced coma to rest his brain. But due to the extent of the brain injury, they couldn't answer the one thing we wanted to know: 'Would he be okay?'

The danger was that his brain would continue to swell, and too much swelling would create too much pressure between the skull and brain. They could operate again and take away more of his skull, but if they had to do that, the best outcome would be that Steve would be alive, but in a vegetative state for the rest of his life.

We couldn't even think about that. We just wanted him alive. We couldn't get the thought of him dying out of our minds. They told us to just concentrate on him getting through the night before they could assess any further damage. They left us then, while we tried to come to terms with what we'd just been told. We tried to remain positive but it was hard. Amy had been texting the whole time, so I went outside to call her. I stood behind a wall, trying to guard myself from the people around me.

I was still trying to hold it together for Mum, but as soon as I heard Amy's voice, I let it all out. 'Steve could die,' I said. She went quiet. I could sense her shock as I told her what had happened. She was the only person I told; I couldn't bring myself to tell anyone else. After the call, I looked up to the sky, almost looking for Dad to give me some support. I couldn't hold back all the questions of why this had happened to us after everything we'd been through. I found myself almost begging for Dad to provide some miracle for us. Steve didn't deserve this. Neither did Mum. I went back into the room and tried offering Mum as much support as she needed. She held it together well, we both did, but there were times when it got too much for us both.

We waited for more news. After an agonising four hour wait, they told us we could go and see him. He was in ICU, a critical care unit with 24/7 support. As we went in, I was mentally preparing myself for the worst. How would he look? And how would Mum react?

The nurse pushed the double doors open and there he was, with tubes everywhere and a white bandage wrapped across the whole of the top of his head. His breathing was being controlled by a machine. It was like seeing Dad after his first accident – a horrible flashback to something I had tried to never think about again.

I held Mum tightly but we both broke down. We stood next to his bed, holding each other close, hardly daring to look. We couldn't bear to see him like that. I tried offering some words of encouragement, saying that he was going to be okay, even though I didn't know if I believed what I was saying. But it seemed to help Mum, and she took Steve's hand in hers and held it tightly. I stood back and just watched my mum cradling my brother's hand in hers. It was too much.

I turned around and let my tears fall. The anger was rising in me and I clenched my fists. I wanted to rail against it, to scream and shout. But I knew I had to be strong. I composed myself. I went to stand next to mum and said hello to Steve, trying to act like everything was going to be okay.

We stood with him for a while and the nurse who was looking after him explained everything that was happening. They were keeping him in an induced coma and closely monitoring the pressure on his brain. If the pressure got too high it would lead to him getting worse, with a strong chance that he would die. The surgeon had done all he could, the machine was breathing for Steve, and they were watching him closely. It was now just a waiting game to see whether my brother was going to live or die.

CHAPTER 18

HANGING TOUGH

Steve managed to get through the night and that gave me just a little bit of hope. I compared Steve's accident with Dad's first suicide attempt, the accident that left Dad in a coma, and I started to feel like Steve could recover, just like Dad had.

But as the hours passed, the signs got worse. The pressure in his head increased slowly. They were holding back from operating and they were trying different medicines to try to stop the swelling, but nothing was working.

We kept on talking to him. The nurses didn't know if he could hear us or not, but we'd felt that Dad had been able to hear us after his accident, and it helped us keep our minds busy. Otherwise, the enormity of what was happening was just too much to take.

I held his hand, just staring at him and silently wishing for a miracle. 'Come on, Steve,' I would say. 'You're so strong, you can get through this. You've always been the stronger brother.'

I could tell that the nurse watching Steve was getting more and more worried. Doctors kept coming in to assess the latest situation, give her some advice, and then leave. It was hard to know what was going on. Finally, she turned to us and said, 'I think you need to stay here tonight, the pressure on his brain is getting much worse.' To me it seemed like she was saying, 'Don't go anywhere; your brother is about to die.' In desperation, we asked if there was anything else they could try. But by now even the option we had originally been given, of them removing more skull to relieve the pressure, was out of the question. The doctor told us, 'It's unlikely that he'll survive being moved to the operating theatre.'

It was getting harder to stay strong, to hold back the emotions, and I knew I had to let them out somehow. I went out to get some air, called Amy, and said, 'They think Steve's going to die.' I could feel the panic rising as I told her what had been happening. She helped to calm me and I managed to slow my breathing down, but I was desperate now. 'This can't happen! He can't die. Is our family cursed? Why is everyone I love being taken away from me?' I managed to calm myself down, wiped away my tears, and said, 'I love you,' to Amy. I went back inside, gave Mum a hug, and stood by Steve's bedside. I stared at him, a tear dropping from my eye. I just wanted him to open his eyes!

I was almost scared to go back in just in case things were worse, but he seemed to be about the same. The continued medication seemed to keep him stable enough to stay alive, but his brain pressure wasn't dropping. All I could do now was to go on believing in my brother. I kept urging him to stay strong. I leant in to him and said, 'You can do it, Steve. It's not your time to go yet.'

Nothing the medical team had been trying had helped to relieve the pressure, so one of the doctors suggested draining the fluid using a spinal tap. It felt like a last chance solution, but to our amazement it worked. The pressure on Steve's brain started to drop. At first, they worried that the fluid was draining too quickly, but eventually they managed to stabilise the pressure. I could sense the relief in the nurse who was looking after him. I could also sense the amazement from some of the doctors who had been trying to save him throughout the day. I don't think any of them really expected it to work.

We didn't know what would happen next, but Steve had pulled through. Somehow, he had made it this far. And in that moment, that was all we cared about.

Steve was kept in intensive care for the next few days. It looked like he was going to survive, but no one really knew how well he'd recover. The brain scans weren't looking good, and doctors warned us that the damage might mean he'd face extreme difficulties for the rest of his life. I tried to deal with that: just how much quality of life was he going to lose? They couldn't tell us whether he'd even be able to open his eyes, let alone remember us, or be able to walk and talk again ...

As the days slowly passed, Steve regained enough strength to be moved out of intensive care with two nurses monitoring four patients. This was hard to deal with. Even though he was still getting 24/7 care and monitoring, not having the sole focus just on him any more made me worry that something bad might happen.

Every day we hoped for signs of improvement, but none came. They reduced all of the medication that was keeping him in a coma, and started to get him breathing with less support from the machine.

Slowly, very slowly, he started to show signs of coming out of it. But when he finally opened his eyes, he just stared blankly. The moment I'd prayed and pleaded for had happened, but it wasn't like I'd imagined it. There was no recognition in his eyes. He just stared into nothingness; he didn't move or respond to anything. It was heartbreaking.

As the days passed, Steve started to show some improvement. He started to react a bit more to some basic tests, and he started to breathe more on his own. They decided to take out the tracheal tube in the hope that he might start responding and talking.

Mum was visiting Steve alone when she rang me. Seeing Mum call me, on a day I hadn't gone to visit him for the first time, scared me at first. Had something happened? I answered in panic, but Mum just said two words, 'Steve spoke!'

There was joy in her voice as she told me what had happened. 'The nurse asked him who I was and he responded, "Mum".' Not only had he been able to speak but he had recognised her – the thought that he might never have been able to recognise her had terrified her.

I went with Mum to see him the next day, still a little fearful that he wouldn't remember me.

'Who's this?' the nurse gently asked him as we approached. 'Mum,' he said. 'And who's this with her?' she asked. Did he know who I was? I could see him concentrating hard for 5–10 seconds and then he said, 'Paul.'

I sighed with relief. But I could see that just saying that one word had been such an effort for him.

As the days progressed, Steve did too. He started to speak more and showed more signs of responding. He still couldn't eat, drink, move, or communicate much, and also there were worries that he couldn't see very well. But every sign of improvement gave us something to hold on to.

We wanted to see how much he remembered too. I asked him what had happened on my stag do and he replied, 'Pepp.' I knew straightaway what he was trying to say – he was remembering the infamous pepper spraying incident in Krakow. Just knowing that he remembered the times we'd spent together, just knowing that Steve was still in there somewhere, even though he couldn't reach out to me, was still such a relief. We had nearly lost him. Just days before we had been desperate for him to open his eyes. This was progress.

As the days turned into weeks, the improvements started to add up. He started to swallow, slowly being allowed to drink and eat solid foods. He still couldn't move so Mum and the nurses had to feed him.

As he continued to improve it wasn't long before it was agreed that he should be transferred to another hospital in London, Homerton, which specialises in rehabilitation after a brain injury. He had to wait a few weeks for a bed to become available though, and they moved him to Southend Hospital in the meantime, which was more local to us. That meant more of his friends could visit him, and they could see the improvements in him day by day. By then he was eating and drinking whatever he wanted. Most days I took him a smoothie and sometimes a treat. Physically feeding my big brother chocolate and helping him drink through a straw were things I'd never expected to have to do, but the fact that Steve seemed so accepting of it made it easier.

Around this time Grandad fell ill too. He was 92, and still very healthy and active for his age, but he was quickly finding that he couldn't do what he used to do. One evening I had a phone call from his doctor to say that I needed to take Grandad in to hospital. I wasn't told much on the phone, but later found out that his recent blood tests had shown that his potassium levels were too high and if it wasn't treated he could have a heart attack. We took him in and they started treating him straightaway. I stayed with him until about 5.00am when he was finally taken to a ward. I was tired, I was drained, and I found myself questioning why, when everything had seemed to be getting back to normal, something else had to happen.

There I was again, sitting in hospital, watching my grandad deteriorate, seeing him looking weaker than I'd ever seen him, while in another ward, about 500 feet away, my brother was still so very broken.

Grandad's treatment worked and he was sent home after eight days. But over the next few months, I found myself in and out of hospital with Grandad, and had to care for him more than ever. My dad was an only child and Steve was in hospital so I felt it was on my shoulders to care for him now. And I was constantly on edge, waiting for the phone call to tell me that something had happened to him. And then I found myself blaming Dad again. 'If Dad was here he'd be dealing with all of this, he'd be looking after Grandad and supporting Mum. He should be here to help with Steve.' I couldn't help it. I started to feel those hateful emotions arise again, wishing he was there to make things easier. I was lucky, I had Mum and Amy to support me, and Grandad's neighbour helped too, because I couldn't care for him alone.

As Steve continued to improve he was moved into a specialist ward that focused on his rehabilitation at Homerton University Hospital. His eyesight still wasn't good, he had no real movement at all, but cognitively he was doing well. We hoped that Homerton would really help him. When I went to visit him, I could see a difference in the treatment straightaway. Steve had a therapy timetable and there were lots of things in place to help him re-learn basic skills.

Some of the patients had similar injuries to Steve, but they had all suffered differently. Steve still couldn't move or see properly, but he was starting to talk and joke like he had done before the accident. Plenty of patients were able to walk around without any difficulty, but they didn't really know who they were. One patient who had been a lawyer in London before his accident walked around the ward thinking he was a doctor. Another, who was in the bed next to Steve, just kept crying. His family said that he had never cried before the accident, but now his brain injury was causing random outbursts of emotions. Another randomly shouted, 'Fucking hell!' every few minutes, but otherwise seemed fine and could hold a conversation.

Looking around at the different patients all suffering with a brain injury, I couldn't help but think back to the mental health unit Dad had been in. Sure, there were obvious differences, but hearing stories of how a brain injury had completely changed their behaviour shocked me. I went home and watched a Ted Talk from Dan Avery who talked about a link between brain injuries and signs of depression, bipolar, OCD, and other mental health issues. He explored the case of two patients who were both showing signs of bipolar and who were given the same medication. A brain scan on each patient told a different story: one had a minor bleed towards the front of the brain and the other had minor damage to the back of the brain. The interesting thing is that based on this scan and this evidence, both patients should have been treated differently.

I thought about Dad's depression and wondered what would have happened if they'd taken a scan of his brain. Would there have been some damage showing before his breakdown? Could the damage caused from his initial accident be a reason why his behaviour changed?

It's surprising how someone treating a patient with potential mental health issues never thinks to look at the brain. I know it will never give a complete indication of exactly what's wrong, but surely looking at the brain should be included within diagnosis and potential treatment of any mental health issue? Every other health practitioner will always look at the body part they're treating. Imagine a broken leg being diagnosed without an X-ray? Imagine a doctor telling you you've got cancer without screening?

Minor brain bleeds and damage from concussion can affect the brain in all sorts of ways; even heading a football can cause long-term damage. The former England football captain Alan Shearer has spoken out about the potential link between heading a football and dementia. Seeing how closely my dad and patients in the mental health unit were behaving in comparison to Steve and other patients around him, all suffering with a brain injury, really made me wonder about potential brain injuries being a cause of some mental illnesses.

Meanwhile, I was worried about Steve. He had been improving above all expectations but now seemed to be progressing a little slower than before. His movement was obviously the biggest issue, and he still had very little movement in his arms or legs. His eyesight was still affected and after waiting for a while on the NHS, Mum decided to take it into her own hands and book a private assessment.

Within minutes of him assessing Steve, he came straight out with it – the diagnosis was wrong. The problem was actually being caused by bleeding behind the eyes. He said that, if it went well, surgery should clear the blood and restore his eyesight. The specialist was so appalled with the misdiagnosis that he didn't charge Mum for the consultation. In fact, he pushed it through on the NHS meaning Steve had the operation within a few weeks. It took a little while for him to recover after the op, but it had been a complete success and Steve's eyesight was completely restored.

I will never be able to appreciate just how hard it must have been for Steve. When I think about the times we'd walk into the ward at visiting hours and see him just sitting there, staring ahead but with blurred vision, just listening to everything around him. I'm amazed at how calm he managed to stay, going through all of that and not being able to move or see. When I hear people moan about trivial things or complain about the weather, I think to myself about Steve and how he barely registered a complaint about not being able to move or see.

It's only when you pause and take a break that you realise just how bad things have been. That's when it really hits you. It went from the high of getting married in Italy, surrounded by loving family and friends, and not being able to wipe the smile from my face, to Steve's accident, seeing Mum broken through it all, and then Grandad falling ill. And just when I thought things couldn't get any worse, my mum's companion, Charlie the dog, passed away suddenly. To some reading this he'll just be a dog, but to my mum he was far more. I'm sure he helped us all keep it together after Dad died. I'll never forget the time the vicar came round to discuss Dad's funeral arrangements. Charlie was only young (and feeling extremely horny) and decided to hump the vicar's leg!

Losing Charlie so suddenly was a huge shock to everyone, and it was a horrible time for Mum. She was dealing with so much pain and still dealing with the life-changing accident her son was going through. Charlie had helped keep her sane. He used to jump on her bed in the morning and encourage her to get out for a walk. And he even became a family confidant – we all loved talking to Charlie! Having to tell Steve was hard too as he loved Charlie. I drove up with Mum later that day and wheeled Steve outside to the park to tell him. He was upset and desperate to see him again, but knew that he never could.

Things were still so hard for us all. But, as was becoming increasingly clear, we were a tough family …

CHAPTER 19

LIVING FOR TODAY

Tough? I'm stronger now than I've ever been. But I can't help but think how I would've dealt with Steve's accident, trying to support Mum, caring for Grandad, and trying to balance a new marriage with running a business, if I hadn't dealt with my depression and focused on my own self-improvement.

How would I have dealt with this years ago? How would Mum have dealt with it if she hadn't overcome what she had too as well? I started to feel grateful that both Mum and I had been through those challenging times and overcome them. Through the adversity I'd developed a strength I never knew I had, and I'm sure she had too.

I look back at the biggest lesson I learnt from Steve's accident and it is simply to live for today.

You hear people say time and time again that your life can change in a heartbeat, but you never expect it to happen to you. Even watching Dad break down and take his own life, I still didn't expect life to change as dramatically as it did for us all. Steve wenttoworkasnormalandnearlydiedbecauseofa"freak"accident. Life is so precious and moments like these make you realise how things can change so suddenly. Just seeing my brother go through what he's had to go through reminds me how grateful we should be for all the things we take for granted every single day.

Learning how to stay present and focus solely on the now is something I'd tried before, but it was only when Steve had his accident that I really had to live it. Knowing that I couldn't change the past and not knowing how Steve would recover, I learnt that staying present is one of the most important things I could do to stay mindful. To stay sane throughout it all.

I've got a more open relationship with Steve now too. We were always close but I often refrained from talking to him about how I was really feeling. Why? Because we are men. And men don't talk about their feelings. Men have to man up.

Not any more. I'm tired of it.

Nearly losing Steve made me realise how silly all that male bravado is. I nearly lost the opportunity to tell him all those things I wish I'd told him before. I nearly lost the chance to spend more time with him. I nearly lost it all. I'll never take our relationship as brothers for granted ever again.

His outlook on life has changed too. 'I'll never stress or worry about work ever again,' he once told me, reminding me just how little our daily worries and stresses actually amount to. He's taught me the importance of acceptance and patience. He has days where he's upset, frustrated, angry, and devastated that this has happened to him, but most of the time he's accepting of it. He knows he can't change what's happened, he knows he's not going to be able to walk any time soon, but he stays patient with his recovery and focuses on improving one thing at a time.

My brother laughs at how many times I've called him inspiring, but there honestly isn't another word for him. I know he's my big brother and I've always idolised him. But this is different from that time I jumped in the swimming pool because I wanted to be like Steve. This is me at 28 years old looking up to my 30 year old brother in complete awe of his recovery and the way that he's dealt with it.

Life's too short to moan about the weather.

CHAPTER 20

OPENING UP
TO THE WORLD

With Steve getting better and family life settling into a happy pattern at home, I started getting back into a work routine. I'd been neglecting my business for a long time and it was time to get back to work. The problem was that my business wasn't really inspiring me any more. It had started off as a passion business but really I had gone into it to make money. Because of this, my motivation was waning and I found myself procrastinating throughout the day, putting off tasks, and just needlessly scrolling through social media.

Something had to change. I'd been feeling this way for a while, even before Steve's accident, but with a wedding to pay for I'd been focusing more on the money I was making than the kind of work I was doing.

Just before Christmas 2017, I made more money from the magazine and from consulting in two weeks than from the yearly salary I'd been on in my first "real" job. (The one I left just after Dad died.) This of course gave me a sense of achievement and it gave me security, but the money felt meaningless to me. It didn't matter that I was making more money than I'd ever made in my online business, there was something missing. I felt like there was more to work than the money I was making.

Maybe I was just getting more mature? Let's face it, my detachment from materialistic items was clear to see as I drove around in my brother's old 2005 Fiesta, even after I'd made over £20,000 in a couple of weeks. The old me would have rushed to the car dealership and got an Audi on finance, but after seeing everything that had happened to Steve, I knew what I wanted to do ...

Two years before, I'd attended an event held by an ex-mentor of mine. As a group we'd done a guided meditation to help us find more meaning and purpose in the work that we were doing. But all I'd been able to think about was my dad, how his death had impacted me, and how I'd managed to turn that adversity into strength. I thought about my depression, how that had hurt me, and where I'd be if I hadn't managed to overcome it. After the meditation, I wrote down just seven words in my notepad:

I need to help people like Dad.

As the day went on I couldn't get those words out of my head. And when the day finished, I got in my car, ready to drive home, and I started to cry. It wasn't normal crying though; I wasn't sad. I couldn't quite explain it. I laughed it off, rolled down the window, turned the music up, and drove home.

I spent the next week working on the ideas that had started forming, and continued to run my business as it was. But I also decided to write an article talking about my dad's suicide. I called it *Why Men Kill Themselves*. It was like therapy to me. I sat there for a good few hours typing away until 5.00am in the morning, telling people my dad's story, and opening up on how I came to forgive him.

The post was for a charity called CALM, which takes a stand against male suicide. After submitting it to them they wanted to publish it on The Huffington Post as well. Between the two sites and my own personal blog, it was seen by close to 50,000 people.

That's when I started to get messages, emails, and comments from men sharing stories of their own struggles with suicidal ideation. And from sisters, wives, daughters, and mums who had lost male loved ones through suicide. As the messages started to come in – and for one of the first times in my life – I felt truly proud of myself.

Although it feels impossibly hard when a loved one takes their own life, and it's hard to talk about it, I wanted to show people that it can be so helpful to reach out to people who can relate to what you're going through. I talked about how I'd reached out to someone after my dad died – the boy at school who had lost his dad to suicide – just so I could try to make that connection.

I wrote a couple more articles after that and published a few videos. I found that writing content about mental health and suicide, from a personal perspective, was a way for me to actually deal with things. Almost like cheap therapy. But even though it felt right, my business mind was telling me something different. It was still telling me to focus in on money.

As the months passed, I started to focus back on the fashion business and consultancy – that's where the attention and, more importantly, the money was. Again, I started to chase the numbers, the video views, the traffic to the website, and the money I was making. I still felt very uninspired creating the content and doing the work I was doing, but I knew that it would pay the bills. More and more though, I wanted to talk about mental health. But talking about mental health isn't sexy. Talking about bespoke suits from Savile Row and the hairstyles that will get you laid is sexy.

It was getting harder to fight the feeling though and with every month that passed, I had the urge to reach out and help people like my dad. I was just too scared to pursue it. I was fearful of being completely vulnerable, of being an open book, and putting it out there for everyone to see.

I was fearful of my dad looking down and being ashamed of me for showing everyone his "so called" weakness and his downfall. I feared that my friends and the people around me would think that I was doing it for attention, and I worried about the negative comments that would come with it. So I didn't do anything ...

But in February 2016, I got invited out to Atlanta to speak at an event called Style Con (now called Menfluential). It was run by YouTubers in the men's style and lifestyle space, and I'd been asked to speak about my work as a lecturer at the London College of Fashion. Originally, I'd been happy to agree to it, I just wanted the platform to speak and meet people, but I knew that I'd struggle to talk effectively on a subject I wasn't really motivated by. A few days later I emailed back asking if I could speak about male depression and my own experience of depression tied into the story of my dad. I knew it would be a challenge to stand on stage and talk openly about it, but I knew I'd deliver a better presentation on something that meant so much to me. They agreed and having never seen me talk in public before, they took a huge chance on me, letting me speak about a topic no one else had touched on – and making mine the last talk on the final day of the event.

I was about to become the most open I'd ever been, and I was about to put myself in a very vulnerable situation in front of over 150 men. It had taken me years to even talk to just one person about it. It had taken me years to openly admit I was depressed and that my dad killed himself. But now I was going to stand in front of everyone and say it out loud.

When the day of my presentation arrived I felt nervous but ready. I was just worried about being so vulnerable. I was worried about people judging me or about completely breaking down like I had done in my hotel room the night before when I practised it. Then, I'd only had to say the opening line and I'd crumbled. I didn't know how I'd react if that happened to me on stage.

I knew that showing some of my true feelings would improve my presentation, but uncontrollable tears and struggling for breath? That would probably be a bit too much.

As I walked on stage, I took a breath and looked around. The audience was perfect for me to deliver this presentation to – they were all looking to better themselves. Through chatting to lots of them the day before, I'd seen that they were open to talking about mental health issues. I looked over to the two guys who had taken a chance on me and invited me to speak. They seemed a little bit apprehensive but also excited to hear what I was about to say.

I introduced myself, looked around the room, and said,

'On the 4th of March 2009, my dad, my idol, my everything, left home, walked to a busy road … and stepped in front of a lorry.'

I delivered my talk a little nervously, but honestly. And I managed to pull through without crying. In fact, afterwards, I worried that I had shown too little emotion. Maybe I just had no emotions left after the floods of tears the night before. Afterwards, a few guys stood up clapping, and once I walked off stage, I started to gather a crowd of people around me wanting to ask questions. Hearing men open up about their own depression, their suicide attempts, and how it felt like I was talking directly to them, was inspiring to hear. One guy broke down in front of me, crying as he spoke about his own depression and suicidal thoughts, and thanking me over and over again for talking about it so openly.

I left the event feeling like that wasn't it. I knew I still had more to do, but I went back to running the business and doing what I'd been doing before.

A few months later, the urge resurfaced. I was fed up with how uninspired I felt and how my motivation for work was the lowest it had ever been. It took a phone call to turn it all around.

I was speaking to a friend I'd met through business about what we were both up to. He could sense how unmotivated I was and he could tell I was lacking the drive that I used to have. I told him about my urge to share my story and my experiences around mental health, and I told him how my fear kept holding me back.

He said, 'You're being selfish, Paul.'

I was confused. 'What do you mean?'

He said, 'By you worrying what people think, by you being afraid that you won't make money, or be able to do this as your work – that's selfish.'

I still didn't get it. So he spelt it out for me.

'Because your story has helped people already. But you worrying too much about yourself isn't helping anyone. You could help so many people by sharing this ...'

That was what I needed to hear. He was right. It was about more than me, it was about much more than my ego, and it was about more than me worrying about what my old school friends or neighbours would think of me and my struggles. That made it easier for me to push through the fear. I started creating the most open and vulnerable content I'd ever created – and I felt inspired by it. Getting motivated every day was easy again. I was enjoying the work I was doing more than ever, and I wasn't chasing money. I was doing it for all the right reasons. *I was doing it because I needed to help people like Dad.*

I started to write more, including working on this very book you're reading right now. I started to put out videos on YouTube, Facebook, and Instagram focusing on mental health and sharing my own personal experiences. I started to document how I was feeling, showing other men that it was okay to not be okay. I started to feel proud of the work that I was doing, and with every message I got thanking me for my honesty I felt more connected to Dad. I felt like I was doing this with him.

This might sound cliché, but being told that a video you shared saved their life is far more empowering than money, or people thinking I'm "cool", or driving around in a fancy car.

It's hard to comprehend how grabbing a camera, hitting record, and publishing my thoughts on mental health and suicide can impact a stranger in such a way. But it goes to show, the more we're open about our struggles the more we can help others. As my favourite quote goes: *Don't be ashamed of your story, let it inspire others.*

CHAPTER 21

MOVING FORWARDS ...

As I write this, my laptop sliding from right to left as I sit on a train heading to London to speak at a mental health event, I trace back through the past nine years and ask myself this question ...

Where would I be and what would I be doing if Dad hadn't taken his own life?

Not a minute goes by when I don't wish my dad was still here. I wish he was by my side now, sitting with me on this train, talking to me about the football, making stupid jokes, or probably just sleeping!

The thought of never physically touching him still gets to me. It's a strange feeling, knowing that there is someone you love so dearly, who you'll never see again. To think that someone you'd say good morning to without a care in the world is now someone you wish was there to say good morning to. I've found myself trying to picture what he'd look like now, nine years on from when I last saw him. Would his hair be more grey? Would he be growing old gracefully? Would he still be going without underwear under his trousers?! I don't think that gut-wrenching sense of loss will ever truly go. And those are questions I'll never be able to answer.

My dad's suicide affected me deeply. It affected our whole family. But what it also did was make us stronger.

As I write this, my brother gets stronger daily. He inspires me every day. Just a text from Mum telling me how well he did at physio can set me off. I honestly can't put into words how amazed I am by everything he has done.

My grandad is 93, and still moaning! He's slowly accepting that at his age, he won't be able to do the things he used to. But just spending time with him really opens my eyes to how important it is to live life in the moment. To make the most of every opportunity while I can. Like he has. Hopefully I'll be there one day at 93, thinking back on what I have done and not what I could or should have done. I don't want to have any regrets; I want to be proud of the life I've led.

Mum surprises me every single day. She's handled everything that's been thrown at her in terms of Steve (which involves everything from getting him washed and ready in the mornings to assisting with every physio session he has). She's still there for me when I need her, just like she always has been, and she hasn't drunk a drop of alcohol for six years.

I remember in my wedding speech, I said that my mum may sometimes look like someone who's quiet, shy, sensitive, and emotional, but inside ... she's the strongest person I know. Her resilience and her ability to get through everything is hard to put into words. She teaches me to keep going when things get tough.

Steve keeps improving. He spent just under a year in hospital altogether before being released home to live with Mum in a new bungalow she rented, all equipped and ready for his wheelchair.

Everyone who reads Steve's notes before meeting him is blown away. He's been called a "miracle" and told that 19 out of 20 patients with his injuries would die, let alone do as much as he can. His recovery has inspired so many people and I'm so proud to call him my brother. In fact, he laughs at how many times I've called him an "inspiration" throughout it all.

Mum has been by Steve's side throughout it all. Literally. As I write this, it's been 13 months since the accident happened. She visited him every day in hospital, and now he's home she's his full-time carer. He has physio daily and continues to surprise everyone with his recovery. He still has a long way to go, but who knows with Steve? Everything he's been told he'll never be able to do again, he's done.

Amy is there by my side, supporting me at every step of this journey. We've just bought our first family home, not the five-bedroom house we were renting, but a chalet. A place that is really ours, and we love it. The house has been renovated from top to bottom, and I have to give Amy credit for how it looks. It's been her vision all along. I've just nodded and shaken my head at decisions that needed making, while she's done more of the hands-on work, with huge help from her family (I always knew marrying into a family of builders would come in handy).

We celebrated our one year anniversary last month, and it was a challenging year to say the least. We both admitted that it hadn't been a fairytale or something you'd see in a movie, but the challenges that came with it only made our relationship stronger. She continues to bring out the best in me, and hopefully I do the same for her too.

My boys are growing faster than I can keep up with. They're now two and nine. I'm so proud of them. They both have unique qualities and I love them for everything they are. With the recent work I've been doing I've been speaking to a lot of parents who've lost their children to suicide, and that gets to me. I look at my children, I see their happy smiles, and I could never begin to imagine the pain someone would go through after losing a child to suicide. My boys drive me forwards – to keep raising awareness and to make sure we do our best for all our children. With Amy's help, I'm confident that we can teach them that it's always okay to talk, and that we're here if they ever need to share how they feel.

I'm not so confident that the outside support would be there for them now if they needed it. I don't think our society is quite built that way yet. But I hope that they will never feel like they have to suffer in silence or feel ashamed for struggling to deal with how they feel. I would never want them to experience the pain Dad must have gone through. Another thought that keeps me going is knowing that I never want them to see me experience the darkness I felt with my own depression. I always thought it was cliché for a parent to talk about the joy their children bring them, but now I know. They brighten up any bad day I'm having. And if I had one wish, one thing I hope they learn from me as a dad, it would be to share. To talk. To understand that knowing how you feel and being able to deal with how you feel doesn't make you less of a man. Being vulnerable makes you strong.

The article I originally posted on The Huffington Post continues to be read and the videos I started to put out are getting more views than ever before. I get on average about 10 to 20 messages from people every single day, sharing their story of mental health or thanking me for talking openly about something other people are afraid of discussing. The feeling I get from being able to help others, just by turning on a camera or writing down some words and sharing them online, still baffles me. I'm just being me and telling my story. I recently looked at how many people have seen my videos or seen one of my posts on social media in the last year. That figure is over two million. Now that doesn't mean two million people have listened, but it goes to show how many people we can potentially impact when sharing our stories via social media.

I recently held a meet-up in London, so I could meet some people in person and tell them more about my story. I invited a few other speakers along too, so they could share the stories of their mental health battles. With just a share on Facebook and Instagram, I expected around 10 people to show up. Actually, 40 people did. Meeting some of the people who my story has impacted in real life is an indescribable feeling.

I've had to work on detachment though as the empathetic me often takes on board every story I hear. I know that I still need to focus on my own mental health, because I've felt it slip on occasions when I neglect myself for others. We all need to know that we can only help others if we help ourselves first.

I'm not a sufferer of mental health, I'm not a sufferer of my dad's suicide. I'm a survivor. I'll keep on surviving for as long as I can.

CHAPTER 22

EIGHT THINGS
MY DAD TAUGHT ME

I was 18, nearly 19, when I lost my dad. Since that day, I've been on a journey. What were the eight biggest lessons I learnt from my dad?

Give to others – philanthropy heals

Dad was always helping others and he showed me that compassion always wins. Both Mum and Dad would always put others first, and that caring personality they both had has rubbed off on me massively. I think Dad's funeral shows how much he gave to others, with so many people there to pay their respects. At times I think his caring mentality and people-pleasing behaviours let him down. He always gave so much to others, and when he was alive, he taught me to care and help others, with no expectations for them to return the favour. (Provided we care for ourselves too, of course.) Compassion and empathy are two of the most alpha male skills I think we can have. That might sound a bit "out there", considering that for many, being an alpha male revolves around what we own, earn, or achieve. But being able to have compassion for others is an extremely powerful trait. My dad taught me that.

Work hard – within limits

Dad was driven. He'd wake up early, cycle to his workplace, work hard, go for a run at lunchtime, continue working, cycle home, and then sometimes run again, all before treating up to four physio clients every evening for an hour each. He wasn't one to complain about working hard and he instilled in me the belief that the things we want don't always come easily. Any lifestyle you want to lead, anything you want to achieve, it all requires hard work. There's a balance too though. I've found myself using work as a distraction many times, but I know that I'm doing it right if I'm working hard to get what I want and knowing when to switch off.

Go all in on your passion projects

Dad chased his passions. He was an avid runner from his late teens, and ran once, if not twice, daily. He trained hard, he tracked his sessions in a red book I still have stored at home, he ate right, and he competed at a good level for his age. I remember seeing him win the annual school road race and thinking, 'That's my dad!' I used to run alongside him sometimes when he was racing, trying to outsprint him but always failing. My dad's obsession with running definitely rubbed off on me. I get obsessed very quickly about something I'm passionate about. Whether it's a new fitness plan, a diet, a business idea, or a relationship. I'm either all in or I'm all out. I learnt from Dad that going all in on something will get you the results you want. Right now, my obsession is to raise awareness around mental health and to do all I can to support suicide prevention. It's a mission I'm dedicated to, obsessed with even, because I don't want people to suffer like Dad suffered.

Sleep more, sleep better

My dad could sleep anywhere and never really had any issues with sleep. Whether it was a short hour as a passenger in the car, on the sofa in the evening, on a plane, or even in the middle of fast forwarding a TV programme, he never had any issues with sleeping. It was only after his breakdown that I learnt just how important sleep is to our mental health. When he was suffering, especially in the mental health unit, he struggled to fall asleep, he struggled to stay asleep, and he struggled with any routine around sleep. He started overthinking it and getting annoyed when he couldn't sleep properly. You know how it is: you wake up in the night and get annoyed you can't sleep, you keep telling yourself you need to sleep, but then that frustration makes sleeping harder. When I was suffering the most, personally I always felt tired and fatigued. I was sleeping too much, mostly. But I wasn't getting good quality sleep. Quantity of sleep is just one aspect of a good night's rest, quality is the other. I definitely inherited the "sleep anywhere easily" trait from my dad, but I also learnt just how important good sleep is for our mental health.

Stay in the present

My dad was saving for an early retirement. His life was going to start at 50. He was going to save enough money to downsize to a mobile home with Mum and take an early pension. That was the plan, but he took his own life six years before that. What can we learn from that? To stay present. My depression stemmed from living in the past, wishing I could change what happened to Dad. My anxiety stemmed from living too far ahead in the future, worrying about situations that I thought would exist. But being present, living in the now, is where I have found peace. Life can change in the blink of an eye. I learnt that from Dad too – and from Steve's accident. So staying present makes me try to enjoy every moment as it happens. It's harder than it sounds, but worth persevering with.

Follow your heart not your head

That was the advice my dad gave me – and the words have stuck with me ever since. My intuition is something I trust. Your heart, your energy, and the way you feel can be so much more important than your thoughts. With this being said, I think they do work hand-in-hand. My heart tells me what to do and my mind rationalises that decision. I've tried to never let my mind take over, shutting down decisions because they pose too much risk. And I think this has helped a lot. I just wish Dad had taken his own advice on board too, perhaps following his heart would have saved him.

Protect and provide for your nearest and dearest

Looking back now, my dad's obsession with work and money was something I wish I could change. All those hours he spent working, making money for us as a family ... I just wish he had spent some of them with us. With Dad now gone and with the thought of never being able to see him again, I'd pay everything I have just to spend another minute with him. But his obsession with work and money all came from his need to protect us, and to provide for us as a family. I had this realisation as we sat as a family of four, in a house I was renting, with a car I was paying finance for. I realised there was nothing there for my family if anything happened to me. I didn't even have life insurance. I'd rebelled against my dad's obsession with money and security so much, that on the outside I appeared to have everything, but on paper I had nothing. I needed to change, to protect and provide for my family. Just like Dad did for us. To find the right balance.

Deal with pain before it's too late

Seeing what Dad went through still hurts today. Some days I can almost see the pain he was feeling, and because of this, I've learnt to deal with emotional pain, not bury it. Feeling emotions, admitting that you're struggling, and talking about it isn't weak. It's potentially going to save you from a life of sadness and maybe suicide. I know it's a bold statement but it's one I stand by. Talking isn't weakness. Being sufficiently self-aware enough to know how you feel and to express it is powerful. My dad seemed to be enjoying life, he seemed to be happy. Even to this day, I question why he did it. I question the pain he must've been burying, because there were no warning signs. I just wish he had found the strength to talk openly and deal with what he had been going through. Choosing to replace our pain with short-term solutions never wins. I know. I tried it. I may have looked strong on the outside, but I was weak and struggling on the inside. And that is dangerous. Please, don't ignore how you're feeling.

CHAPTER 23

MAN ALIVE!

Way back at the beginning of this book, I asked some questions about our response to suicide. I'd love to know how you'd answer those questions, but for now, here's my take on it:

Isn't it time we did something about it?

It still baffles me that not enough is being done, in spite of everything that we know. Remember those statistics? The ones telling us how many men are already taking their own lives and how that number is set to rise? Now remember that they're not just digits on a page … they're real lives. They're men. Men with families and friends, and every suicide affects so many more people.

This book – it's just my story. It's how I struggled to deal with it all. It talks about the impact my dad's suicide had on my entire family, and all of the friends whose lives were touched by my dad. But with 84 men dying from suicide every week in the UK alone, we know that this problem affects far more people far more deeply than we'll ever be able to comprehend.

The more you think about it, the more shocking the statistics sound. Because when you think about it, you can't stop thinking about the pain those men must have felt. You can't stop thinking about the desperation they must have experienced, feeling like their mental pain was so great, so unconquerable, that it compelled them to take their own life ... that's what's truly shocking.

On the positive side, more is now being done to bring these statistics into the limelight. Awareness around male suicide is growing and awareness around depression in men is increasing too, but more still needs to be done for prevention.

It's not just about suicide risk, it's about mental health in general. The support needed isn't easily accessible. But it should be. This isn't a small problem. Let's remember: suicide is the biggest killer of men under 45. It is the biggest killer of young people. The suicide rates among young women are rising too ...

This isn't a small subculture of people asking for more to be done. This isn't a small amount of people being affected. Depression is killing us. It kills someone every 40 seconds. We need to shout about this – and go on shouting – until more support is put in place.

You wouldn't have this with any other illness. Especially a physical illness. If a physical illness was killing as many people as depression, more funding, research, support, and prevention methods would be put in place to stop it from happening. It would take time, but it would happen.

But with mental illness? With depression?

How many more people need to die by suicide until something is done?

As I jumped into raising more awareness for mental health issues, I started to have more open conversations with people, many of whom have experienced feeling suicidal. I've spoken to many who have attempted suicide, and they all say the same thing:

'Help came when I hit rock bottom. Help came when I attempted to take my own life and failed.'

It's not good enough. I keep hearing story after story like this – just like my dad's story – nine whole years after everything that we went through. Why hasn't there been a bigger, more visible change in how depression is treated.

We can't go another nine years without doing anything. Heck, we can't go another year without doing anything. We need to start trying to help with depression (and prevent it when we can) before it gets too late. One of the biggest lessons I've learnt from my dad's story is that when our perception of life darkens, when it feels like life is closing in on us, and we can see no way to end the mental distress, it leaves people facing one single, stark question:

Do I try to survive another day, or do I end this pain?

I know that change won't happen overnight. This isn't something that one man alone can change, but together, we can change the way mental health is seen and treated. Together, we can stand up to suicide.

Do we really need to "man up" and get a grip ... or should we actually "man down" and change the way we deal with our emotions?

Man up? Man down? Is there even a right answer?

Through writing this book even my opinions on how men should deal with emotions has changed. I was team "man up" for a long time, realising that the image of what a man used to be is a far cry from the reality of what a man is today. But trying to persuade men to "man down", be more in tune with their emotions, more sensitive and open, doesn't work for everyone. What is important is knowing what works for you. It's knowing what kind of man you need to be for your loved ones.

If we try to force one or the other, we end up dictating what it takes to be a man. We end up trying to force men to be something they may well fight against. It's all about balance.

I look at my grandad, aged 93; he's experienced things that I and a lot of men in my generation would've struggled to get through.

139

That stiff upper lip attitude towards not needing to talk or cry in order to deal with his feelings has served him. And it's served so many other men like him ...

But me? I tried it. It didn't work. I wore a mask and tried to front it out, to pretend I was dealing with it "like a man", while inside I was being torn apart. I needed to talk, to cry, to start focusing on what made me happy in order to be able to deal with it. Everyone is different. A lot of how we're brought up by our parents defines how we deal with things. And that's why having that self-awareness is so important to getting through things.

I know that I shouldn't be ashamed of showing my vulnerability, to cry if I feel like crying, or talk openly about my struggles. I know that what I own or earn doesn't define me as a man. But at the same time, I know that lifting heavy weights, protecting and providing for my family, competing with others, pushing myself daily, and taking risks also serves me as a man. Oh, and eating steak too!

It's all about balance and self-awareness – making up your own definition of what it takes to be a man and living to that definition.

Something definitely needs to change – men should feel able to talk to other men about how they feel. The suicide rates within male-dominated environments show that. It has been said that construction workers are three times more likely to take their own life than the rest of the population. It shows that there's still a taboo around men talking about mental health issues, and that needs to change.

Society needs to change, and that's something that won't happen overnight. It's a generation thing. My great-grandad influenced my grandad in what it took to be a man, and he influenced my dad. My dad influenced me and, consciously or not, I'm already influencing my sons. *My sons* are looking to me to determine what it takes to be a man – and that's quite a responsibility.

All I know is that the current way most men are dealing with their mental health isn't working. The suicide statistics show that.

Is there even a right or wrong way of managing how we feel?

You cannot put depression into a box. It doesn't discriminate. No matter your age, gender, race, upbringing, academic achievements, and career success, depression can strike anyone. Therefore, there's no "one size fits all" treatment.

This is certainly what needs to change: antidepressants and other medications are readily available, but other treatments aren't. I could go into the doctors this evening, explain that I'm feeling low, and be prescribed a pill that works to balance chemicals in my brain affecting my mood and emotions. But to see a therapist? I'll probably have to wait months for that. There's a huge reliance on antidepressants and medication to make us feel better when we're in dire need of help. But pills alone aren't enough.

Recovery takes time. And everyone deals with past trauma and depression differently. I first dealt with it by bottling it up and replacing those sad feelings with short-term pleasures: the clubbing and the alcohol, the fancy car and the expensive clothes; they only ever helped to numb the pain. But that never lasted long. What helped me was opening up: talking. But more importantly, understanding and forgiving. I also owe a lot to the reading I did, the exercise, and the change in what I ate and drank, alongside practising mindfulness and doing something purposeful for my work. But for others, those solutions might not work. Everyone has to find their own route to recovery. But the good news is that there are so many things that can help us. We just have to try as much as we can to realise what will work for us.

A classic example of that played out the other day. As a moving in present, Amy and I were given a 1,000-piece puzzle. There are a lot of articles out there saying how puzzles can help you switch off and can help with mindfulness. I guess sitting down and doing a puzzle does help you to stay present. As we sat down together to do the puzzle, she looked excited at the prospect, whereas I looked less than thrilled. Around 30 minutes passed. Amy was in her element, putting together piece after piece, and with each piece she became calmer and more present. I, on the other hand, was still struggling to place a single piece and was getting more frustrated as the minutes passed. Amy spent a few evenings after that completing the puzzle. I didn't touch it again. It made me frustrated, and it seemed to take how I felt and make it worse. But Amy was visibly calm, present, and peaceful. There are so many things out there to help us handle how we feel; it's all about finding what works for you.

Try as much as you can. Find what helps you and use that as a tool for when things get tough. No one thing will solve depression. But a combination of things will help us recover.

All in all, there is no right or wrong way to deal with how we feel ... the main thing is that we do deal with it.

CHAPTER 24

JOIN MY JOURNEY

I don't want this conversation to finish and I'd love to keep it going. I want us all to be able to talk openly about mental health, to normalise the conversation. I currently share daily on social media, whether that's on Facebook, Instagram, LinkedIn or Twitter, just search for "Paul McGregor" and you should be able to find me.

To share your story and to let me know your thoughts on this book, you can contact me through my website too: **www.pmcgregor.com**

I'd love for you to join me on this journey. To break the stigma that surrounds mental health. To show others that it's okay to talk and, of course, to stand up to suicide.

In the space of nine years, I've gone from someone who lied about how my dad died because I feared judgement, to now sharing daily on social media and in as many places as I possibly can, because, well, I need to. It inspires me every day, knowing I can help someone like Dad to live another day.

My dad could still be alive. My dad should still be alive.

I can't do this alone, I'm no saviour. I'm just someone who wants to share my story to hopefully inspire others to do so too. Because the way mental health is seen and treated will take years, if not decades, to change, but we have to start somewhere. If you're with me, let me know. Let's keep this conversation going. Speak soon ...

Instagram: @pmcgregorcom

Twitter: @pmcgregorcom

Facebook: /pmcgregorcom

AFTERWORD

Since this book first went to print, figures were released suggesting that male suicide rates had gone down. More new figures may have been released by the time you read this. But, whatever the rates are showing, and whatever the latest trends, we can't ever afford to be complacent. We can't overlook the fact that men are still three times more likely to end their lives than women. As I'm writing this, it has also been revealed that teen suicides have risen sharply. That is a sickening thought. But I remain hopeful. And as long as we keep talking about this, we will make a positive difference. We can win this fight, together.

ACKNOWLEDGMENTS

I wasn't the only one affected by my dad's suicide; this is just one story, one internal dialogue of many.

Mum, this book may have been difficult to read, but through everything that's happened it's now clear to me that you, through everything you've been through, are the strongest person I know. I owe so much to you – too much to put into words. Everything I do, everything Steve does, is a result of you. It's a result of how you brought us up and how you continue to be there when we need you. Thank you. I love you.

Steve, my dedication 18 months ago would've been very different. It would've been mostly based around bad jokes and banter, but after everything you've recently been through, it only seems fitting to say how proud I am to have you as a big brother. Being able to look up to you throughout my whole life is something I'll always cherish. And the last 18 months have shown me just how lucky I am to have you as a brother. They've shown me just how strong you are mentally. You were and always will be my best man. Keep inspiring. Love you, bro!

Amy, you helped me through dark times in ways you'll never know. At a time of darkness, you were the light that came into my life. I'll never forget that. You've always brought out the best in me and continue to support my dreams along the way. I couldn't wish for someone better by my side. I'm proud to call you my wife, the mother of my children, and my best friend. Here's to many more exciting years as husband and wife. I love you.

Freddie, I've loved seeing you turn into the boy you're becoming, and I can't wait to see you turn into the man you will become. You've brought so much joy to us all and ever since you came into my life, you've been the reason why I've wanted to become better. Everything I do, I do it with you in mind. Here's to many more Lego sessions and bike rides. I can't wait to be with you as you grow up.

Teddie, when you're old enough to read this, you're going to find out a lot about your grandad. You're going to see his downfall, but you're also going to see just how loving he was as a dad. I wish you could've met him, but more importantly, I wish I could have the same effect on you as he had on me. You've added so much joy and meaning to my life, and I can't wait to see you grow up. I will be by your side. Every single day.

I also want to thank my grandad. I'll always cherish our time together, even though it now normally involves moaning! At 93, your attitude towards life is something I try to match.

Thank you to my nan. I would've loved for you to be a great nan to the children.

To my friends who've consistently made me laugh and supported me, to family friends who helped us through the dark times, and also to every single one of you, everyone who has read this book, watched a video of mine, messaged me, or simply liked a post of mine, you inspire me to do more. Every single day.

Also thank you to Chris for working with me on this book and correcting my grammar on multiple occasions. Chris and the whole Trigger Publishing team have been a pleasure to work with.

Finally, thank you to Adam Shaw. You emailed me two years ago after reading that first blog post I published, telling me to turn my story into a book. Now you've helped make that happen. Thank you.

**If you found this book interesting ...
why not read this next?**

Daddy Blues

Postnatal Depression and Fatherhood

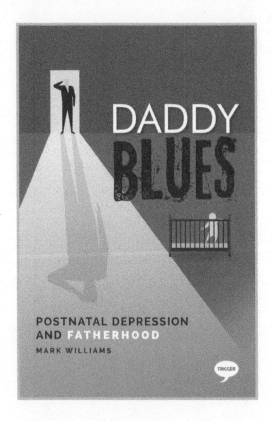

Mark Williams knew of the baby blues for mothers,
but he never thought it might happen to him. And then it did.
Daddy Blues explores a story we all know from a
different perspective.

Running with Robins

Bereaved, Not Broken

When Gemma's dad died, she continued
his hobby of running in order to feel closer to him –
but then she took it too far ...

Barber Talk

Taking Pride in Men's Mental Health

Following his friend's suicide, Tom Chapman
decides to use his barber skills for good and make a
difference to the state of men's mental health.

EXTRACT FROM BARBER TALK

CHAPTER 6

RIP ALEX

That day in 2014, my conversation with Alex went a little something like this.

'Hey! How's it going?' I asked.

'Not so bad, thanks,' Alex replied.

'Did you have a good time away?'

'Yeah, it was really good.'

'I've got to get back to work, buddy. My lunch break is over.'

'Yeah man, no worries!'

'See you.'

'Later, mate.'

Now, I'm not saying that this was our exact conversation – I'm sure there would have been some reference to wrestling in there. But it didn't consist of much more than that.

'Well, it was nice to see Alex – I'm so glad he had a good time away,' I said to my workmate as we made our way back through Torquay town back to my salon, Tom Chapman Hair Designs.

Little did I know that it was going to be the last time I would see Alex before he took his own life.

A few nights later I jolted awake. I had just been drifting off when I noticed a lot of activity on my phone. Normally I would read on my phone in bed to try to clear my mind of the day's goings on, but I hadn't noticed anything odd. Now, though, Facebook notifications were flying in rapidly. I had to check out of curiosity, but when I saw what was causing all the activity, my heart sank.

There it was. "RIP Alex."

It rushed over me – that feeling of uncertainty and panic, where your chest feels like it's going to implode. I broke out in a cold sweat.

I saw the same comment again, from someone else.

"RIP Alex."

And again.

"RIP Alex."

And again.

"RIP Alex."

I didn't want to believe anything just yet. I frantically searched for a sign, some confirmation that Alex was alive. I wanted to know that this was all a mistake, or a rumour that had got out of control on social media. But the only confirmation I found was that he was no longer with us.

He had ended his own life. It was suicide.

I felt empty. I didn't want to believe it. Someone so young, someone so close to home, and someone so *fun* couldn't be gone! My heart raced and adrenaline rushed through my body; it was similar to that feeling when you have a heated confrontation when you're young.

The news was spreading like the plague; it travelled like a wildfire among all of our friends online. The response was devastating.

Questions began hurtling through my mind as I sat up in bed.

If I had known that he was struggling, would I have paid more attention? Would I have given him more time?

Should I have been more aware, so that I could have realised what was going on?

Should I have given him more time to talk to me?

Could I have made a difference?

Why did he end his life?

What was he thinking when I saw him?

What was he thinking as he jumped?

With slightly awkward and sweaty digits, I tried to message those I knew from our teenage friendship group. I got hold of a couple of people who were obviously in as much shock as I was. They were clearly upset, judging by the typos in their rushed, erratic writing, full of grief and worry.

"He hasn't been happy for ages."

"I heard it was because of love life."

"Why didn't he say anything?"

"I think he was lonely."

"We should of done something, his poor family."

"I think it happened yesterday."

"I have no idea why heed do this he was fine the other day?"

No one I spoke to seemed to know what had happened, especially because, like in many of these situations, (especially online, where news can travel fast) there is a tendency for misinformation. Unfortunately, I don't think any of us will ever know why he did it. I just wish he hadn't. He was the first of our age group to go, and it was way too early.

I was in shock and feeling a certain level of guilt, as I had only seen him days before. I hadn't done anything for him – I hadn't even realised that there was anything wrong. We'd spent time together in the past and shared a love of wrestling, but despite our friendship, I still couldn't see what he was going through.

Why couldn't he tell me he was struggling? I don't necessarily mean that he should have told me something in that brief meeting during a lunch break, but why not before that? Why couldn't we have talked about this via an online message, text, or phone call? Why couldn't he speak to *anyone*?

Or maybe he did try to speak to his friends or family. Maybe he did try, but we all missed the cries for help.

the *Shaw* mind
FOUNDATION

Creating hope for children,
adults and families

Sign up to our charity, The Shaw Mind Foundation

www.shawmindfoundation.org

and keep in touch with us; we would love to hear
from you.

*We aim to end the suffering and despair caused by mental
health issues. Our goal is to make help and support available
for every single person in society, from all walks of life. We will
never stop offering hope. These are our promises.*

TRIGGER™

The mental health & wellbeing publisher

www.triggerpublishing.com

Trigger is a publishing house devoted to opening conversations about mental health. We tell the stories of people who have suffered from mental illnesses and recovered, so that others may learn from them.

Adam Shaw is a worldwide mental health advocate and philanthropist. Now in recovery from mental health issues, he is committed to helping others suffering from debilitating mental health issues through the global charity he co-founded, The Shaw Mind Foundation. www.shawmindfoundation.org

Lauren Callaghan (CPsychol, PGDipClinPsych, PgCert, MA (hons), LLB (hons), BA), born and educated in New Zealand, is an innovative industry-leading psychologist based in London, United Kingdom. Lauren has worked with children and young people, and their families, in a number of clinical settings providing evidence based treatments for a range of illnesses, including anxiety and obsessional problems. She was a psychologist at the specialist national treatment centres for severe obsessional problems in the UK and is renowned as an expert in the field of mental health, recognised for diagnosing and successfully treating OCD and anxiety related illnesses in particular. In addition to appearing as a treating clinician in the critically acclaimed and BAFTA award-winning documentary *Bedlam*, Lauren is a frequent guest speaker on mental health conditions in the media and at academic conferences. Lauren also acts as a guest lecturer and honorary researcher at the Institute of Psychiatry King's College, UCL.

Please visit the link below:

www.triggerpublishing.com

Join us and follow us ...

@triggerpub

Search for us on Facebook